Plant Hire
for
Building and Construction

Plant Hire
for
Building and Construction

H. T. MEAD
and
G. L. MITCHELL

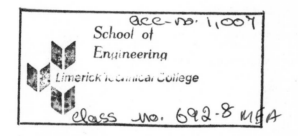

LONDON

NEWNES-BUTTERWORTHS

THE BUTTERWORTH GROUP

ENGLAND
Butterworth & Co (Publishers) Ltd
London: 88 Kingsway, WC2B 6AB

AUSTRALIA
Butterworth & Co (Australia) Ltd
Sydney: 586 Pacific Highway, Chatswood, NSW 2067
Melbourne: 343 Little Collins Street, 3000
Brisbane: 240 Queen Street, 4000

CANADA
Butterworth & Co (Canada) Ltd
Toronto: 14 Curity Avenue, 374

NEW ZEALAND
Butterworth & Co (New Zealand) Ltd
Wellington: 26–28 Waring Taylor Street, 1

SOUTH AFRICA
Butterworth & Co (South Africa) (Pty) Ltd
Durban: 152–154 Gale Street

First published in 1972 by
Newnes-Butterworths, an imprint
of the Butterworth Group

ISBN 0 408 00080 5

Filmset by V. Siviter Smith & Co Ltd, Birmingham

Printed in England by Fletcher & Son Ltd, Norwich

Preface

In this manual our intention has been to assist building and civil engineering contractors in the determination of the economics of their trade. We have not described and categorised contractors' plant nor have we attempted to indicate capacities and capabilities of machines. Where references have been made to equipment by type, such as excavators, cranes, etc., it has been the intention to give examples in generic rather than specific terms.

Information for the book was collated during an unstable economic period, and, therefore, it is quite probable that the financial position may have changed drastically by publication date. Inevitably this means that although the theory be sound the figures themselves may no longer be representative. This, however, will in no way affect the validity of their application, because their relativity will still be in proportion.

Naturally, there will be differences of opinion, particularly between manufacturers, contractors and plant-hiring companies, on many points. Depreciation percentages vary considerably, but we have used the Inland Revenue amortisation calculations as these are the yardstick which industry has to follow whatever internal arrangements individual companies wish to make. Similarly, when purchasing plant, bulk and contractual arrangements alter the situation and again we have based calculations purely on 'one-off' purchases. In addition, current CPA rates are used when illustrating the cost of hiring. We cannot assess the ideal utilisation periods or discounts that may be given. Any deviations of this nature are for the individual companies to incorporate.

At the present time the building and construction industry is in the process of changing from Imperial to metric (SI) units. Some manufacturers and materials producers have been producing specifications showing metric equivalents for some time, although the industry as a whole is not familiar with the system. Accordingly, we have quoted costings and performance examples in what we consider to be the most easily understood terms within context and have included, at the end of the final chapter, a list of useful conversion factors.

H. T. Mead
G. L. Mitchell

1971

Acknowledgments

The authors acknowledge with gratitude the assistance and courtesy of the many sources without whose help this book could not have been prepared. Among the individuals and companies who have given their time, advice and, in many cases, have permitted extracts from technical papers and manuals, special thanks are due to:

Atlas Copco MCT AB
Barber Greene (England) Ltd.
Mr Magnus Bergman
Caterpillar Tractor Co.
Clark Equipment
Contractors Plant Association
Mr. Colin Hammersley
Institution of Mechanical Engineers
International Harvester
John Blackwood Hodge & Co. Ltd.
Mr. A. E. Lakin (Scottish Aggregates Ltd.)
Mark Thomsen Ltd.
Massey-Ferguson
Montague Kent & Co. Ltd.
Pumpcon Ltd.
Richards & Wallington Industries Ltd.
Mr. Russell Jones (H. Leverton & Co. Ltd.)
Terex GM
Wickham Engineering Co. Ltd.

Contents

CHAPTER ONE

The Plant-Hire System

It is extremely doubtful whether there are any industries in which planning is more critical, relevant or vital than in the construction industry. It is equally uncertain whether any business runs more closely to the borderline of success or failure than that industry. Right through the process from job analysis, tendering procedure, project management and final completion, the profit or loss situation is vulnerable. It will always be in jeopardy unless every step of the process is handled with the utmost care and accuracy, and nowhere along the line is the profit in more danger than in the operation and utilisation of mechanical plant.

Perhaps it is not always readily appreciated that the construction industry is the world's greatest business. It is responsible for earning more money and for employing more labour than any other single industry. Therefore, by virtue of the influence that it must exert both on a national and an international scale, it has an enormous responsibility to be economically viable, whether on the smallest type of building, a single domestic unit, or on the construction of a major project of the vast proportions of the Tarbela Dam.

It seems extraordinary, therefore, that many users of civil engineering and building plant and machinery are grossly unaware of any figures relating to the equipment, other than those of capital cost and fuel consumption. Fortunately for the construction industry the larger and more efficient firms, as well as the equipment manufacturers, have in recent years been doing a good job in educating those other members of the industry by teaching them the importance of evaluating the costs of every single item of plant they use and for every minute of the day they have it.

Of course, every contractor is conscious of the fact that the downtime of machines is the biggest profit-sapping item on his books, but just how much each machine costs him during each phase of

1

operation is not always appreciated. Therefore, it is not easy for him to make an accurate assessment of how to plant-up for a job and to decide whether it is more profitable to purchase the equipment out-right, to hire in, or rent, or to take the alternative of hire-purchase through a bank loan or a finance company.

In this respect, full acknowledgement should be paid to organisations such as the Construction Industry Training Board in the United Kingdom and its counterparts in continental Europe and the USA. They have done sterling work in educating the plant user, and it is regrettable that the CITB should have found itself in difficult times in the course of it.

Obviously, the contractors have been motivated to acquire this knowledge by sheer necessity and the manufacturers and their distributors were not slow to appreciate that it was as important to themselves as to the industry they are serving to increase efficiency this way.

In the years since World War II, the UK has seen a growth of plant hire for the construction industries that is nothing short of phenomenal, and this has flourished under conditions of economic stress which have not affected the construction industry nearly as much as was originally expected. All of which tends to indicate that the plant-hire business has been entirely beneficial to the industry. In fact, about one-third of the plant employed in the construction industry in Britain is supplied by plant-hire companies, and in the early 1970s over £50m worth of equipment was bought annually to hire out. Most of it is British made or made in Britain under licence and is in addition to the increasing amount of foreign equipment being brought into the country to satisfy the need. The business was stimulated, of course, by the financial situation in the country when investment and credits were not readily available and, therefore, the risk of holding capital equipment was consequently reduced.

Many other factors influence the situation and several of these will be discussed under different headings in the ensuing pages. But this aspect of the exigencies of a national economy must not be over-rated in the contractor's assessment of whether to buy or to hire. There are many other relevant factors that will be of more immediate concern. For instance, a contractor is not going to buy in as a stop-gap measure if a piece of vital equipment has broken down or if he is under pressure to meet a contract deadline; nor is he going to purchase when his credit is only under stress temporarily. These are ideal conditions favouring plant hire.

As a rule-of-thumb guide it can be said that if plant is going to be used for more than a year it is worth buying, but for less than that it is cheaper to hire.

The Alternatives

When a contractor needs to acquire mechanical plant he has various courses of action open to him. He can purchase outright, he can call in a plant-hire company (rental), he can obtain extended credit from the manufacturer, he can negotiate hire-purchase or he can lease the equipment through a bank or finance house. Which method he prefers is entirely dictated by the nature and length of the work for which plant is required and the current status of the company. It may be that the machine is needed for a short time while a vital stage of the contract is being handled, or perhaps to ease a temporary financial embarrassment. Possibly the contractor needs to use the machine and cash in on its residual value, or perhaps he does not want to be involved with the machine on his books. Each decision has its own merits. In fact, one of the obvious benefits of any form of rental or leasing is that the user has no need to keep records of wear and tear for depreciation and tax purposes.

If he hires (or rents) the plant it comes with an operator and usually he has only fuel costs to meet after the rent; if he adopts hire-purchase, the title to the plant is vested in his company; if he leases, the title remains with the finance house.

Some UK manufacturers who deal direct with contractors and not through distributors or agents for home sales, normally require settlement within 30 days and for periods in excess of that arrange for the business to be conducted through a finance house. Some of them offer the additional service of credit sales, whereby they accept 20% of purchase price prior to delivery and spread the balance over up to two years with quarterly or half-yearly repayments.

Government-Backed Exports

In Britain, manufacturers exporting equipment and services receive considerable support from a Government source known as the Export Credits Guarantee Department (ECGD). Under the ECGD terms the manufacturer, having satisfied the Department with evidence of the customer's creditworthiness, can arrange a direct loan to the overseas customer, who pays 10% down with order, a further 10% with the shipping documents and 80% of the purchase value loaned by the bank. This loan is underwritten by the ECGD, who will reimburse the bank in the event of default of payment. Of course, the ECGD require very strict evidence of creditability of the client and in effect the loan is virtually made to the client's country of origin rather than to the company. Under this ECGD scheme loans can be either long or short term, extending up to five years.

The ECGD agreement, when extended, is an assessment of the market rate of the customer's country and a flat charge is made for the credit which is not related to the period involved and the amount of credit required. For short-term credit, 30 days up to and not including two years, the facility charge is usually $\frac{1}{8}-\frac{1}{2}\%$ over current bank rate and ECGD terms generally give overseas credit up to two years for sums of about £15 000–£20 000, but for larger amounts of, say, £80 000–£90 000 it may extend credit to three or even five years for buyers. For distributors, however, the terms are limited to two years. Other countries have their own schemes to assist their exporters but opinions of British manufacturers favour the UK system. Virtually all banking houses have a large interest in the financing of plant and equipment. Many have wholly owned subsidiary companies, while others have extensive holdings in other finance companies. In each country they operate differently, although within each country their terms but not their rates of interest may vary. It is the variation in terms that makes it advisable for the customer to shop around. The terms will all depend on how badly the finance house wants the business.

Hire-Purchase and Finance Leasing

The two most common ways for a contractor to obtain equipment, other than by plant hire or by outright purchase, are by hire-purchase or by leasing (more correctly known as finance leasing). The main deciding factor in choosing between the two is the taxation benefit to the customer which will always be governed by the current state of his company. There is no strict definition by which one can state that one method is preferable to, or cheaper than, the other. Using standard actuarial tables it is possible to make a case for both methods and to show each to be cheaper than the other. It is all a matter of individual company conditions at any given time.

In hire-purchase, the customer has to put down a substantial deposit and make regular repayments over an agreed period and with the option to buy at the end of that period for a small nominal sum. The equipment becomes his and the finance company has no interest in it. But with finance leasing the finance company never relinquishes title to the equipment. The customer selects the machine, the lessor buys it and the customer pays one rental in advance and uses it for an agreed period, say three, four or five years, without the option to purchase. In the hire-purchase method all repayments are allowable against tax and in leasing all the rentals are tax deductable. At the end of the lease period he usually has the option of continued rental at a reduced price, usually something like $\frac{1}{2}$ % of the cash price of the machine. Also, after the initial period he may elect to hand in the machine, in which case he can benefit from the proceeds of sale or part exchange against a new machine. This will all be handled by the finance house.

A variation on these two common methods of obtaining equipment is the contract-hire system, sometimes called 'leasing-off-the-top', in which the supplier undertakes to buy back at a guaranteed price after an agreed period. This method, unlike the other two, involves a greater maintenance surveillance to ensure the good condition and retained valued of the machine. This, of course, limits the customer's selection of equipment because of the fewer manufacturers prepared to guarantee buy-back terms.

Systems in Switzerland and Sweden

In Switzerland, most of the financing is undertaken by the banks rather than finance houses. There a manufacturer takes the customer to the bank and when the contract has been agreed the buyer reimburses the bank in half-yearly instalments, at about $7\frac{1}{4}$–$8\frac{1}{4}$%, over periods ranging between two and five years.

In Sweden, leasing is not widespread but it is more popular than the plant-hire system. When plant hire does operate it has certain factors in common with the UK system, i.e. the agreement covers replacement, wear and tear and includes an operator where necessary, but unlike the British system there is no organisation similar to the Contractors Plant Association governing hire. Generally, this system is limited to machines such as earthmovers, compressors and pumps. It does not cover the very wide range of all equipment as found in the UK and does not include plant for asphaltic work, batching, cranes, etc. It is a private agreement between the two companies.

The Swedish leasing system is for the most part in the hands of five or six banks, each of whom has a separate company solely for leasing. Typical of these is the Svenska Handelsbanken and under the service they offer the contractor orders his equipment from the manufacturer, the bank pays for it and the contractor makes regular repayments. In the event of default the bank usually will re-sell the equipment back to the manufacturer. The usual term is for five years but, three-, four- and six-year contracts can be arranged. Banks admit that the interest charged in Sweden today is high, but they are reluctant to quote figures.

During the period of leasing, the banks endeavour to maintain supervision over the equipment concerned. It is not usual for them to employ their own engineers for this and to some extent they have to rely on the manufacturers for this service. For the most part the banks find that their business is done with the small to medium-sized contractors and their business is on the increase. Regrettably this is not so much a sign of a rising demand due to increased construction work, rather it reflects the current lack of capital.

The larger contractors, such as Svenska Cementgjuteriet, tend to buy all their equipment in hard cash. Large earthmovers are depreciated over a five-year period, while excavators are written off over seven to eight years. At the end of that time the contractors usually trade in their equipment, expecting to realise 7–10% of the original purchase price.

Some manufacturers are known to give up to two years' extended credit, charging smaller contractors about 11–12% interest, but this does not seem to be recognised by the banks, for they deny the existence of this sort of operation in Sweden.

Continental Reluctance

When it is so obvious that plant hire has been successful in the UK, both from the plant-hire companies' and from the contractors' point of view, it is difficult to understand why other countries have been so slow to appreciate its advantages.

On the Continent, plant hire is still something of a rarity. Many European firms do not take easily to the idea of even just hiring the equipment, not to mention the equipment *and* the operator. And in the USA, plant hire operates under completely different conditions. Why should this be so? The answer still eludes many people who have spent a long time in the industry and no one has a quick general answer.

Germany and Switzerland

One possibility is to consider national traits. Germans, for instance, tend to be extremely possessive by nature as, indeed do the Swiss. They just simply do not like to have anything that they do not own and have not paid for outright. They take pride in paying for something before they use it and then they continue to use it, even though it may not be the type of equipment best suited to the job nor the most economical. But even this does not seem to be entirely satisfactory as an explanation. It may be more relevant in the case of the

Swiss contractors but in Germany in the post-war period they have gone through considerable fluctuations in the building and construction industries and they, more than anybody, know how to go broke on a contract. It is not many years since German contractors were going through the bankruptcy courts at a frightening rate. In early 1967, in the first three months of the year, more contractors went bankrupt than in the whole of the preceding year. This was due very largely to the manner in which contracts were being placed by the authorities. They were small and piecemeal and there was no assurance of continuation of work—certainly not admirable conditions for a healthy construction business.

With these conditions, and with foreign manufacturers frequently offering attractive purchasing terms at low interest rates extended over long periods, it is not surprising that many German contractors were burdening themselves with costly equipment and little likelihood of renewed contracts to justify the capital outlay. The result was that the contractors were working on a ridiculously low profit margin. It was reported at the time that they were working on the same contract prices as obtained ten years previously, because of the high competition that was generated over these small contracts—the contractors were frightened of making a loss on the plant they had purchased and of losing their trained operators. As the recession worsened the vast amount of foreign labour that had been imported into the country to meet the boom period of a few years before began to circulate madly, striving to sustain a work record in order that their visas should not become invalidated, and skilled plant operators resorted to labouring to retain some place in the only business they knew. None knows better than the German contractors how important it is to keep skilled equipment drivers constantly employed on their machines to get maximum productivity when those machines are required—and the prevailing conditions worried them considerably.

Those, surely, were the ideal conditions for the growth of plant hire. But it did not happen. Neither are there more than slight signs now, although it is widely recognised that it must come one day.

Under such conditions the industry itself cannot prosper nor can the manufacturers who supply it, for they can neither expand nor invest in research and development for the future. Furthermore, when it is the country's greatest industry, the whole economy is adversely affected. Fortunately, however, that period of recession in Germany did not last too long and by 1969 the whole economy was in an enviably healthy state and the construction industry shared in that revival—only to hear, once again, rumours of recession in late 1970 and 1971.

Holland and Sweden

Similarly, at the end of 1967 and the beginning of the following year, Dutch contractors were finding the going hard. The number of cases of bankruptcy in the building industry was rising and the industry as a whole was faced with the necessity for more efficient and responsible financial management, and from that could not be divorced the need for another look at plant purchase and utilisation.

In Sweden, there have been signs of increased interest in the hiring business. As yet only slight signs but, at least, they are renting small equipment such as pneumatic tools, compressors and space heaters and it may be assumed that it will not be long before this acceptance has spread in volume to excavators, crushers, graders, cranes, loaders and all the rest of the range of heavy earthmoving equipment. Perhaps they may even see the benefits of the British system of hiring not only the equipment but the drivers with the equipment.

France

In France a sort of hire-purchase system operates in some cases where the manufacturers are prepared to let their machines out to users for 'trial periods' before the final purchase is entered upon, and this virtually constitutes hiring prior to subsequent outright purchase with guaranteed buy-back terms. But the slow acceptance of the hiring system is probably due, in the main, to the strong influence of regionalisation on all forms of construction. There they regard the money that is to be spent on, say, a length of highway as having been gathered locally and, therefore, that it should be spent locally.

This often means that contractors tendering for a job, or part of a job, are selected as a result of their suitability and their stability, being judged in local terms. This is indicated by the size of their plant holding (even if it is limited to, say, a 2 m³ sized loader, a mobile crane and a couple of rear tipping trucks). Conversely, it is assumed that they are not capable of doing the job if they are unable to show evidence in their plant yard of the necessary equipment. Frequently, such ownership is taken as prima facie evidence that the contractor is not only financially stable but that he has had previous experience in the type of job being discussed. Again it becomes obvious that the equipment is going to be used irrespective of its suitability for the work in hand.

This is not the case, of course, with the many large and internationally operating construction companies who have nothing to learn about efficiency in costing, but it does apply to that vast number of small contractors and builders who form the backbone of the industry. Talk to most owner–operators and they can tell you immediately just how much their machines cost initially. They can also tell you how much fuel they consume and how much they pay their operators, but there the story ends. Ask about depreciation, hourly cost, downtime cost, and the rest, and frequently they have no idea of the sums involved. In fact it is not unknown for them not to know how much profit they are making on a job! This is indicative of the room for education that exists in such areas.

Expansion of Plant Hire Abroad

A particularly significant year, however, for the expansion of plant hire abroad seems to have been 1969. It began to expand in Scandinavia, especially in Sweden, opened up in Belgium, and made a start in the Netherlands. Even in France it seemed that more interest was being taken—but no more than that. The extraordinary thing about it all was the vast extent of ignorance that still existed (and probably still does exist) about the operation. In a visit to the Fédération Nationale des Travaux Publics, in Paris, one would be shown with pride films of most of the impressive civil engineering projects carried out by the country, and on the journey to, and through, Paris the building of the Boulevard Periphérique and the Metro extensions were tribute enough to French contractors' ability. How this could all be achieved by companies with management (and that after all is where the decision is made to hire or buy) so ignorant of how the plant-hire system had grown and worked only a few miles away across the English Channel is a mystery. At that time, in 1969, there were between six and twenty (no one was quite sure just how many) slipform pavers standing idle in France, and contractors' plant yards were well stocked with outdated, depreciating plant. This was the time that the French Government took the decision to acknowledge the fact that year after year their autoroute building programme had fallen two-thirds short of the target of 300 km per year. While Germany had built over 4000 km of autobahnen and Italy had over 3000 km, France still had fewer than 1000 km. The answer was found in the Government saying that their next two major autoroute contracts would be awarded to contractors prepared to undertake the financing. The contractors would have to put up 50% of the finance, while 25% could be raised by bond issue (or similar) and the Government would contribute the remaining 25%. The most potentially successful contractor would be the one which would require the Government to put up no money at all. In any case it was made amply clear to the contractors that they could not expect to receive the Government's portion for two or three years.

Obviously, the answer to these conditions lay in the formation of a large and influential consortium consisting of major highway contractors, and their efforts are expected to produce more than the 300 km per year and a total of 5000 km by the early 1980s.

This has, of course, meant that they could start their offensive with a lot of newly-purchased plant and a great deal of outdated plant that they just could not afford to throw away. With the large stocks of plant involved in such a huge programme of scheduled continuity one might well expect to see the growth of large plant holdings by the consortia concerned and, in order to sustain modernity and to justify the outright purchase of specialised equipment, these conditions should lead to the hiring out of temporarily low-utilised plant to other contractors engaged on construction and maintenance of non-autoroute classification and on urban motorway building and maintenance.

At that time of critical planning, the heads of the Fédération Nationale des Travaux Publics were in ignorance of the way the British system worked. They did not have a ready-made expression equivalent to 'plant hire' but used 'l'occasion de matériel', a literal but obviously unfamiliar equivalent.

At the same period, discussions with German contractors revealed the same unfamiliarity with the system. Furthermore, both contractors and some of the larger manufacturers' dealers were in ignorance of the system of guaranteed buy-back. This is such an integral part of the understanding and operation of plant hire that it must be absorbed and appreciated before commencement of any operation involving hiring, renting, leasing or buying of equipment. When learning of manufacturers in the USA and the UK who were prepared to guarantee predetermined buy-back rates against the purchase of new plant in two or three years' time, the German contractors initially showed open disbelief which later turned to considerable interest, indicative of a possible pressure of demand which may be brought to bear on manufacturers later in this decade.

There can be, in superficial discussion in Germany, misunderstanding about the term 'plant hire' even today. Some contractors think that plant hire is used in the Federal Republic but, in fact, what they mean is that often a small contractor will undertake to operate on a sub-contracting basis, particularly for earthmoving. Because this kind of operation involving time, quantities and cost factors is sometimes undertaken by contractors with outdated plant it has inevitably given rise to the opinion, in some quarters, that only failing firms will carry out this work. This certainly is not always the case but the impression still persists in some instances. It is an indication that there is still room for education within the industry. However, during 1971 there have been reliable reports that plant hire was to be found, albeit rarely, in Germany on lines similar to those in Britain, whereby equipment could be hired for building and construction complete with operator and even with rates in special categories to allow for periods of transportation and erection (in the case of crane hire) charged at a different rate from that applicable to period of utilisation. It may therefore be assumed, with reasonable confidence, that Germany will follow Britain's lead in this respect.

American Practice

As was stated earlier, the American hire or rental system differs considerably from what is common practice in the UK. While not being indicative of how the entire system works throughout all types and ranges of building and civil engineering machines it may, nevertheless, be useful to study it in relation to the portable compressor business.

Most compressor manufacturers build compressors in the following ft^3/min sizes: 85, 125, 150–160, 250, 365, 600, 900 and 1200. The standard psig of these compressor sizes is generally 100. Most specifications will state that the compressor should produce, say, 85 ft^3/min at 100 psig.

More recently, several companies have introduced machines in capacities other than those mentioned above. Joy Manufacturing has introduced a 100 ft^3/min machine. Sullivan has introduced a 750 ft^3/min machine, and LeRoi has introduced a 450 ft^3/min machine. The capacities of portable compressors are generally arrived at as standard models in terms of how many air tools they will run or how many blast-off valves, etc. Some of the smaller companies, such as Lindsay, offer compressors smaller than 85 ft^3/min; however, these are very much in the minority.

Contrary to general practice in the UK, very few users in the USA of the small-sized machines (250 ft^3/min and smaller) will specify diesel engine drive. CP offer a 125 ft^3/min machine with either gasolene or diesel, as well as a 160 ft^3/min machine and a 250 ft^3/min machine with gasolene or diesel. All their machines in excess of 250 ft^3/min capacity are standard with diesel drive and this, of course, is also standard in the industry. As the cost of operating a diesel-engine-driven compressor is less than a gasolene-engine-driven machine, most companies will rent this equipment at a slightly higher rental price for the diesel machine when there is a choice of gasolene. In the large machines, the complete power is diesel, as mentioned above.

It would be difficult to estimate how many distributors there would be in the USA but in all probability every worthwhile construction equipment distributor would have an air account in addition to his other accounts. And it is almost a certainty that every distributor who has an air account will lease or rent equipment such as portable compressors.

There are also a considerable number of small rental houses which rent but do not sell. This is the type of house where you might rent a portable saw or a portable snow thrower, or something similar. Generally speaking, these houses will rent only the small machines up to the 125 ft^3/min capacity. They are not interested in selling equipment, whereas the normal construction equipment distributor is very much interested in selling the equipment and uses the rental business as a means whereby rentals applied to the purchase price of the machine will make it attractive to the user to purchase the machine.

Rental prices vary from section to section in the country. No two areas are really exactly the same, and usually the price at which the rentals are made is the amount the market will bear. In large metropolitan areas, such as New York, the general rate is $1.00 per foot of capacity; thus a 600 ft^3/min machine would rent for $600 a month. The Associated Equipment Distributors' rate for a 600 ft^3/min machine is certainly not $1.00 a foot. For example, the CP book rate for a 600 ft compressor is $150 per month, which is subject to a 20% distributor discount. But it is unlikely that they, or any of their competitors, ever get the $850 per month rate in renting compressors.

The length of the rental also has very much to do with the final price. For example, there are daily, weekly, and monthly rates and usually the daily and weekly rates are considerably higher than the monthly rates. The longer the rental period, the lower the price. Also, while the large machines (600 ft^3/min or larger) may go at somewhere near $1.00 per foot, the smaller machine (such as the 125 ft^3/min machine) might go for as high as $1.40 per foot.

Another question to be resolved is the matter of who will pay freight to deliver the machines to the job sites and also to get the machines back to the distributor's place of business. Normally, this would be negotiated, there being no set trend as to who pays freight rates.

When a distributor rents a compressor, what he says in essence to the user is: 'we are giving you a piece of equipment which will produce so many cubic feet per minute of air on an eight-hour-a-day basis'. If the machine does not perform satisfactorily, the distributor and/or the manufacturer must make certain that the machine is repaired and put back on the job so that it actually is available for an eight-hour day of operation. Incidentally, in this respect there will also be different rates for double- and triple-shift operations. By and large, the double-shift rate is one-and-a-half times the single-shift rate; the triple-shift rate is twice the single-shift rate.

The warranty really does not apply in rental equipment. The rentor provides machinery which he purports will do the job and the user is really not that much concerned with a warranty.

Growth of Plant Hire in the UK

The birth of the plant-hire industry in Britain was around 1932–34 and from humble beginnings it has grown into a multi-million pound business, changing and adapting with the fluctuations of the country's economy and consequent demands of building and construction.

The many years of acute shortage and stagnation in design undoubtedly had an adverse effect on the industry. Many with the means to do so indulged in random plant purchase, safe in the knowledge that, regardless of whether the plant enjoyed a high utilisation factor, they could rely on very high residual values, in many cases in excess of the original cost.

During this period, the contractor and plant hirer vied with each other for possession of new equipment. It was inevitable, however, that many old machines had to be used and hired out, creating, justifiably or otherwise, a degree of prejudice towards the use of hired plant.

Significantly, and exemplifying the industry's adaptability, 1968 was a difficult year for Britain. It was off to a start with devaluation in the previous November and then saw the introduction of tariff reforms, revised forms of value added tax, import levies and all the rest of the measures taken by the EEC members to stabilise their own situation. All of which gave the construction business the jitters and resulted in 1968 being probably the most interesting and challenging year in the history of plant hire. Competition increased savagely— for instance, rates for a 100 ton crane fell from £25 per hour to £14 per hour—and several of the less substantial companies were forced out of business by such conditions. Hardly surprising, when at that time municipal authorities owed £500m to developers and building contractors in Britain. Share prices increased amazingly, profits in plant hire climbed and some high-powered take-overs materialised. The difficulty of raising capital at that time (and the sums required to finance plant hire are considerable) meant that larger companies had less trouble in that respect and could borrow cheaper. At the same time the severity of competition forced smaller firms into mergers and often resulted in economies.

New Development

Those turbulent years of 1968–70 also saw the emergence of another development in Britain. A company was introduced with the backing of a demolition and excavation specialist which was well experienced in plant hire. Trading on current money scarcity, high interest rates and the fact that money spent on plant hire earns full tax relief, it put forward a scheme for plant-hire planning. This meant a break with tradition and conventional methods of supplying plant only to the user's specific requirements. Believing that frequent errors of judgement are made in specifying equipment, and that users are not always as familiar with current equipment changes as the plant-hire specialists, the new company undertook to advise on plant for any given project, to visit sites and discuss with management problems of mechanical and materials handling techniques, earthmoving and anything else. On that basis a hire scheme would be prepared and costed. Equipment would be transported to the site and a mobile team of specialists made available to minimise downtime. So far there was little new in that. What was unusual was that further visits were offered throughout the duration of the contract and advice given on reassessment of the plant required to meet the changing nature of the project. It is puzzling why this scheme was not more enthusiastically welcomed by contractors. The concept seemed good but response was not encouraging.

Design Improvements

Of course, job evaluation has always been a major part of what plant hire has to offer—after all, sound job analysis is a concomitant of plant purchase and is offered by major equipment manufacturers—and plant hirers are more and more becoming specialists guided by the reliability and versatility of their experience. From their own point of view, diversification is expensive and that must be reflected in their rates to the user. It also means that specialisation heightens their anticipation of the problems the user will encounter. Knowing the symptoms and behaviour patterns makes prior ordering possible and downtime limited. Much of this, naturally, is the result of communication from the users, which is fed back to manufacturers and, thus, influences the design and modifications embodied in future machines.

Significantly, in 1968 more than 30% of all the equipment produced by member companies of the Federation of Manufacturers of Construction Equipment was purchased by plant-hire companies and they claim to have greatly influenced design philosophy by the advice from their field engineers. That is not surprising when plant hirers, if properly organised, should aim at a full 80% utilisation factor from their equipment, compared with the 10–20% sometimes obtained by too many contractors (a deplorably low figure). So, obviously, makers listen to advice from these plant hirers and tend to use the industry as a proving ground for their products, and the contractors often use the hired plant before committing themselves to purchase, free from pressure by the manufacturer.

A Pitfall

It should not be assumed from the foregoing that everything about plant hire is good. It is no more faultless than anything else in this world. One of the most dangerous pitfalls for the unwary contractor is the rogue or pirate firm whose existence, though shortlived, is a hazard to the contractor and a blight on the industry. There have been small contractors who would undertake deferred term purchase of their equipment for a specific job and either the work dissolved away from them or they could not sustain the repayments. They would then hire out the plant to cover the cost of the repayments. Such rates would therefore be well below the recognised hire rate and appear attractive to the prospective client. In such circumstances, if the machine ran into trouble there would be the immediate difficulty of obtaining spares and service and the contractor would find himself in the embarrassing position of having to turn to a bona fide plant-hire company to get him out of trouble. He learns by bitter experience that, with the kind of arrangement he entered into, there is no guarantee or service contract and that he has no protection.

Rates of Hire

The Contractors Plant Association in Britain and the Scottish Plant Owners' Association in Scotland, have been very largely responsible for the degree of order and respectability that plant hire enjoys in the

UK today. Without it the industry, emerging as it did in conditions of uncertainty, could not have succeeded so well nor rendered such a service—and the construction industry would have been the poorer for the lack of it. Apart from unifying the plant-hire firms, codifying terms and conditions of contract, the CPA has become the arbiter of rates of hire, and even though their recommended charges sometimes bear little resemblance to the rate eventually charged they do form a basis for negotiation. Other considerations, such as competition, length of hire, time of the year, weather and availability, all affect the market. Generally speaking, all hire charges are based on an 80% utilisation factor by the lessor which, while ideal, is not always achieved. Should this factor fall to, say, 60% then there is a temptation to reduce the rate. That is why there is no such thing as 'fixed' hire rates. They are always no more than 'recommended' rates and are always negotiable.

Throughout the plant-hiring business there is found a genuine desire to keep hire rates at a proper level. There are generally considered to be too many low rates available, offered by individuals operating on a low cost, no overhead basis, without costing into their business allowance for depreciation, or insufficient margin for expansion and other necessary factors.

The point should be stressed that rates of hire should be adequate to provide for correct maintenance of the machines, proper training of the operator, capital for supplying the necessary services behind the plant, advisory services, and all the other factors. The only way a plant-hire company can offer an efficient service is by ensuring that the hire rates are good, fair and reasonable. Anyone can seek and get cut-price rates, but he takes the risk that the machine may not turn up on time at site, or that it may break down and be left without spares and replacement service or speedy repair. Nevertheless, it is still possible for the contractor to shop around among the recognised and wholly reputable hire companies and obtain 'favourable' rates, and this is accepted as part of the natural cut and thrust of competitive business. The factors governing and influencing this are, of course, understandable. Availability, demand, importance of the customer quantities, length of period of hire and time of year are all considerations that lead to rate differentials. The plant-hire industry is a sophisticated business these days, even though it may be a very young one, and it would be wise for any contractor to remember that, although it may not always be infallible in other walks of life, never will it be found to be more true than in this industry that 'you get what you pay for'.

Applicable rates are subject to many influences and they do reflect general conditions both in industry and in the country as a whole.

When there is plenty of work about for contractors then the rates tend to climb. When the national economy slumps and finance becomes scarce the demand for hire machines rises and again a rate rise reflects the conditions, but the variations do not occur from day to day, week to week or even month to month.

Things that take effect are items such as the cost of labour, the cost of machines and spares, and office administrative costs such as postage, employment tax, etc. Increased costs in these directions rose 18.75% in 1969–70, reported some plant-hire companies, but their rates to customers did not rise in direct proportion. They do insist, however, that a reasonable rate of return is maintained to ensure that they stay in business and give to their customers the required standard of service, twenty-four hours a day, seven days a week, and often employing radio equipment to call up mechanics to service hired machines that have broken down on highway or on site. All these items have to be costed in.

Brass-Plate Firms

The Contractors Plant Association in the UK currently stands at about 1000 member firms, which is a surprisingly high number in so small an area. Additionally, there are throughout the country numerous 'brass-plate' firms. These are small, often one-man registered companies holding no plant whatever, operating from a one-room office with a telephone and with a brass plate on the wall outside. Despite this description, such companies are not scorned by the CPA and its members for they do perform a service valuable to the contractors and to their larger colleagues in the plant-hire industry. Probably there are 1500–1600 plant-hire firms operating in Britain at the present time.

In some circles the belief is held that too many of the plant-hire firms suffer from poor management. Although they may be good plant men, some directors and managers tend to spend too much time in the workshop instead of involving themselves in the real business of management and the delegation of authority. And that is where the brass-plate men fill the need for they, conversely, are more management orientated and more business-minded. Because they have the stimulus of need and are not hampered by the organisation and plant depot responsibilities and distractions that shackle their bigger colleagues, they are more inclined to go out and seek the work. They spend more time searching the market for what is available and placing it with the construction companies. The construction companies, similarly, are glad to have this sort of agency to turn to when their customary sources are not available to fill what may be sudden, urgent requirements on site.

So there we are, everybody is happy. The contractor gets his plant quickly, the plant-hire companies let machines out that might otherwise be idle in their yard waiting to be located, and the brass-plate man gets his percentage on the deal—usually around the 20% mark. Of course, the rate and conditions to the hirer are the same as they would have been had he negotiated directly with the plant-hire firm and the guarantees of service, operator efficiency and maintenance are unaffected by this system. Although the company hiring out the machine is getting less profit it is, nevertheless, utilising its plant under conditions in which it might not have been working at all. And, anyway, as rates are flexible, who is to say whether the usual effects of supply and demand do not apply equally as well when the contractor is in a tight spot, looking desperately for a machine that he has been unable to track down through his usual channels. Almost certainly the contractor is in a position of some pressure and welcomes the chance to get his hands on the plant as soon as possible. The savings of a closely negotiated price are secondary to the cost of delays on site.

Rising Hire Rates

Some idea of how hire rates can be expected to rise in the foreseeable future, commensurate with all other costs, was given in April 1971 when the Chairman of the CPA voiced its concern over rising costs and their obvious repercussion on hire rates later in the year. The association's survey into basic operating costs is shown in Table 1.1, on the following five pages. The data used to compile the statistics cited were collated from the actual experience of leading firms in the industry and are expressed as representative basic operating figures which are within the range of costs of all operators of these machines. The CPA emphasised that no element of indirect over-heads had been included in the survey and these vary very widely. The operator costs are based on civil engineering London superior grade rates current at the time.

Table 1.1

Operating Costs

		Drott B100 (with 4 in 1 plus cab)
		3 years
		£
Manufacturer's 1971 price		4 800
HP interest, say 7% p.a. over 3 years		1 000
Maintenance, labour and materials		1 500
		7 300
Less resale value		1 000
		£6 300
Divided by 1 600 hours per annum use		4 800 hrs
per hour (machine)		£1.31
operator working (40 weeks)	£0.88	
operator off hire (12 weeks)	£0.21	£1.09
Total cost		£2.40
Comparable figure on a December 1969 exercise		£2.05

		22RB (ICD) (*Crawler crane with 90 ft boom and fly jib and complete crane equipment*)		
		5 years		7 years
		£		£
Manufacturer's 1971 price		12 300		12 300
HP interest, say 7% p.a. over 3 years		2 580		2 580
Maintenance, labour and materials		3 000		4 250
		17 880		19 130
Less resale value		4 500		3 800
		£13 380		£15 330
Divided by 1 600 hours per annum use		8 000 hrs		11 200 hrs
per hour (machine)		£1.67		£1.37
operator working (40 weeks)	£0.90		£0.90	
operator off hire (12 weeks)	£0.22	£1.12	£0.22	£1.12
Total cost		£2.79		£2.49
Comparable figure on December 1969 exercise		£2.39		

	JCB 3C *(type)* *(Hydraulic excavator with one bucket)*	
	3 years £	5 years £
Manufacturer's 1971 price	4 750	4 750
HP interest, say 7% p.a. over 3 years	1 000	1 000
Maintenance, labour and materials	1 400	2 000
	7 150	7 750
Less resale value	1 250	750
	£5 900	£7 000
Divided by 1 600 hours per annum use	4 800 hrs	8 000 hrs
per hour (machine)	£1.23	£0.88

operator working (40 weeks)	£0.88		£0.88	
operator off hire (12 weeks)	£0.21	£1.09	£0.21	£1.09
Total cost		£2.32		£1.97

Comparable figure on December 1969 exercise	£2.05

Note: Assumed annual usage 1 600 hours.

	Caterpillar 951A *[1½ yd³ (1·15 m³)* *capacity multi-purpose* *bucket plus cab]*
	5 years £
Manufacturer's price (last in production 1970)	9 650
HP interest, say 7% p.a. over 3 years	2 030
Maintenance, labour and materials	3 000
	14 680
Less resale value	2 000
	£12 680
Divided by 1 600 hours per annum use	8 000 hrs
per hour (machine)	£1.59

*operator working (40 weeks)	£0.92	
*operator off hire (12 weeks)	£0.22	£1.14
Total cost		£2.73

*Operator—see separate table for breakdown.

Note: Assumed annual usage 1 600 hours.

The above machine ceased production during 1970 and the current replacement machine is understood to be the Caterpillar 951B, now costing £10 974 with multi-purpose bucket, teeth and cab.

	Hy-Mac 580C [*Hydraulic excavator* *with a* $\frac{5}{8}$ yd^3 (479 litre) *bucket*]	
	4 years	
	£	
Manufacturer's 1971 price	9 490	
HP interest, say 7% p.a. over 3 years	1 990	
Maintenance, labour and materials	2 100	
	13 580	
Less resale value	2 300	
	£11 280	
Divided by 1 600 hours per annum use	6 400 hrs	
per hour (machine)	£1.76	
*operator working (40 weeks)	£0.91	
*operator off hire (12 weeks)	£0.22	£1.13
Total cost	£2.89	

*Operator—see separate table for breakdown.
Note: Assumed annual usage 1 600 hours.

The above information relates to the Hy-Mac 580C model, which is still in general use, and not to any later models.

	Pennine 2 [30–35 *ton crawler crane—* *air operated—with* 120 ft (36·6 m) *boom and* 30 ft (9·1 m) *fly jib and* *complete crane equipment*]	
	7 years	
	£	
Manufacturer's 1971 price	18 100	
HP interest, say 7% over 3 years	3 800	
Maintenance, labour and materials	4 500	
	26 400	
Less resale value	8 000	
	£18 400	
Divided by 1 600 hours per annum use	11 200 hrs	
per hour (machine)	£1.64	
*operator working (40 weeks)	£0.95	
*operator off hire (12 weeks)	£0.23	£1.18
Total cost	£2.82	

*Operator—see separate table for breakdown.
Note: Assumed annual usage 1 600 hours.

Operator Cost

	Caterpillar 951A	Hy-Mac 580C
Basic rate (based on London Super Grade)	43p	43p
Addition for operator (plus rate)	6½p	6p
	49½p	49p
Basic week (49½ × 40)	£19.80 (49p × 40)	£19.60
Maintenance (49½ × 10)	£4.95 (49p × 10)	£4.90
	£24.75	£24.50
Graduated State Pension	£0.64	£0.64
National Insurance + SET	£2.15	£2.15
Holidays with pay (w.e.f. April 1971)	£1.25	£1.25
Training levy	£0.15	£0.15
Statutory holidays (32 hrs × 49½p)	(32 hrs × 49p)	
52 weeks	£0.30 52 weeks	£0.30
Employers liability insurance	£0.50	£0.50
Subsistence	£7.00	£7.00
	£36.74 per week	£36.49 per week
=	£0.92 per hr =	£0.91 per hr

Off Hire (12 weeks per annum)

	Caterpillar 951A	Hy-Mac 580C
Basic (12 weeks × £24.75)	£297.00 (12 weeks × £24.50)	£294.00
Graduated State Pension (12 weeks × £0.64)	£7.68 (12 weeks × £0.64)	£7.68
National Insurance + SET (12 weeks × £2.15)	£25.80	£25.80
Holidays with pay (12 weeks × £1.25)	£15.00	£15.00
Training levy (12 weeks × £0.15)	£1.80	£1.80
Statutory holidays (12 weeks × £0.30)	£3.60 (12 weeks × £0.30)	£3.60
Employers liability insurance (12 weeks × £0.50)	£6.00	£6.00
	£356.88 per annum	£353.88 per annum
	£8.92 per week	£8.84 per week
=	£0.22 per hr =	£0.22 per hr

	Pennine 2
Basic rate (based on London Super Grade)	43p
Addition for operator (plus rate)	9p
	52p
Basic week (52p × 40)	£20.80
Maintenance (52p × 10)	£5.20
	£26.00
Graduated State Pension	£0.70
National Insurance + SET	£2.15
Holidays with pay (w.e.f. April 1971)	£1.25
Training levy	£0.15
Statutory holidays (32 hrs × 52p)	

52 weeks	£0.32
Employers liability insurance	£0.50
Subsistence	£7.00
	£38.07 per week
=	£0.95 per hr

Off Hire (12 *weeks per annum*)

Basic (12 weeks × £26.00)	£312.00
Graduated State Pension (12 weeks × £0.70)	£8.40
National Insurance + SET (12 weeks × £2.15)	£25.80
Holidays with pay (12 weeks × £1.25)	£15.00
Training levy (12 weeks × £0.15)	£1.80
Statutory holidays (12 weeks × £0.32)	£3.84
Employers liability insurance (12 weeks × £0.50)	£6.00
	£372.84 per annum
	£9.32 per week
=	£0.23 per hr

Importance of Non-Digression and Anticipation

The really wise plant-hire company is one that clearly defines its method of operation before going into business, basing the conclusions on sound management and experience and, having laid down its guidelines, stays within those parameters. Too many companies have failed to be completely successful because they have allowed themselves to go chasing other imagined profit-spinning activities. Sometimes those activities look very attractive and it takes a lot of experience to be firmly resolved not to digress from the main business of hiring plant. For instance, if someone comes into the office and says that a certain machine is needed for a year's work, it can be a great temptation for the hire company to make a special purchase of that machine. But that is the start of bad practice and it should be stopped before it begins. That sort of procedure and train of thought is perniciously accumulative and before long there will be other diversifications to detract from the main line of business. Few of them really pay off as expected.

Another similar form of temptation lies in the sale of secondhand, or used, plant. Once you get into the trap of selling off used equipment, that side of the business begins to take over. It involves additional paperwork and clerical staff and at least one administrator and a salesman. Then there are demands on the workshop staff, space and time. The machine that starts off by just needing a spray coat of paint before long develops into a major stripdown and parts replacement for which the plant yard was not devised. This is necessary because of the need of the company to keep faith with the purchaser and to guarantee the condition of the equipment. If such practice is permitted to grow, the company will soon discover that the tail is wagging the dog and the plant-hire side of the business is taking second place to secondhand sales—and that was not what the company was formed for in the first place. Far better for the company to obtain its trade-in value agreed at time of purchase and leave disposal of used plant to the manufacturers.

It is also very important that the plant-hire firm should balance its fleet against weather and changing economic conditions, and it is not an unwise move to include within the fleet of large and costly earthmovers, cranes, drilling rigs, etc., a holding of small, well-chosen, inexpensive items like bar benders and croppers. These can pay handsome dividends when sometimes the rest of the fleet is not being fully utilised.

There is absolutely no substitute for sound management training coupled with business acumen born of continual contact with and knowledge of the construction business and its requirements.

Maintaining contact with both the construction and the manufacturing sides of contracting is essential, for this is the only way to forecast trends in equipment demand and availability. At the time of writing, there is one such plant-hire company which, although in business for only twelve months or so, is showing good progress and profitability by following this course. True enough, it is part of a well-known, major contractor's group but, nevertheless, this is not the reason for its success, although undeniably it must be a comfort should business go flat, and it must imbue customers with some confidence. But without leaning on that connection, that hire company has a utilisation factor well in excess of 80%. It has followed its initially prescribed course of trading in plant hire without deviation into any of the other activities mentioned, but just the same has been astute enough to retain flexibility in market assessment. For instance, it has foreseen the developing trends in self-propelled vibrating compaction equipment, acknowledging that towed vibrating rollers have probably reached the end of their development and that the future progress will be the greater in the field of self-propelled machines. To that end it has brought a unique machine to the UK from the USA. That machine is the RayGo

Figure 1.1. *Specialised vibrating self-propelled roller—an example of advanced thinking of plant-hire companies putting unusual plant at contractors' disposal (courtesy John Laing and Son Ltd.)*

$14\frac{1}{2}$ tons self-propelled vibrating compactor, the heaviest in the country—and the first (Figure 1.1). Also, the company has been quick to appreciate and stock the twin-engined self-loading scrapers of the Michigan 100H-T type, which are still new to the European continent (Figure 1.2). These scrapers, although impressively

Figure 1.2. *This* 12 m³ (16 yd³) *elevating scraper was the first of its kind in a UK hire fleet. Working on topsoil removal on a multi-million pound motorway earthmoving contract, it was an example of heavy construction plant being hired in by the contractor from an owned subsidiary hire company (courtesy Elstree Plant)*

demonstrated in all kinds of difficult soil conditions, with a degree of ground adhesion and traction unequalled by conventional scrapers, have not been accepted with alacrity by the contractors. Even their proven success in the USA has not convinced the British contractors. But they must become one of the most important and integral parts of the successful contractor's fleet on earthmoving contracts of any size, and the plant-hire company has been ahead of the game in anticipating the demand.

The same sense of anticipation has been responsible for including in its fleet mobile hydraulic platforms used on short-term work, ranging from maintaining street lamp standards and working on buildings and structures, to repair and maintenance of high-slung direction signs over motorways. They sell for about £20 000 and hire rates approximate £8–£50 per hour. They compare very favourably indeed with the costs of erecting scaffolding and paying for the labour time involved. For short-term hire they are invaluable to the contractor and remunerative for the hiring company, because of their mobility and ready availability for use elsewhere either by the same user or another.

A further example of thinking ahead of the conventional terms of plant hire also would include helicopters—not for personnel but for plant, equipment and materials to sites with difficult access. Such a move, unusual in 1971, will probably become commonplace by the end of the decade for plant-hire companies, although helicopters are not likely to be a regular item of contractor-owned plant for other than personnel carrying.

Where necessary, urgently required replacement parts may be flown by specially chartered aircraft to keep the contractors working with minimum downtime.

CHAPTER TWO

Why Hire?—Why Buy?

Contracting in present-day circumstances demands a realistic approach to the financial consequences, and the factors determining the choice of whether to hire or buy are most important when tendering for a contract. An organisation must ensure the most effective use of its funds, including provision of the most suitable available plant, transport and equipment for carrying out contracts efficiently and economically. Selection of plant and the decision of what to purchase and what to hire is a vital and important decision when estimating for a contract bid. There are many aspects to consider and the ultimate aim must be to achieve the lowest overall cost in the shortest time per unit of work performed.

When planning a contract, consideration has to be given to hourly operating outputs and costs—the unit cost per cubic metre, per ton or per square metre is the arbiter rather than the capital cost of a machine. When planting a contract there are four sources of supply: (a) from existing plant holdings; (b) purchase of new plant; (c) hiring-in from a plant-hire organisation; (d) leasing from the manufacturers (or bankers).

If the value of the job is high then there is no doubt that all four sources of supply will be used.

A further source is the sub-contractor who could be used for any number of jobs. The trend today, in the UK, is to use the latter method wherever possible. By doing this the main contractor off-loads a lot of the detailed humdrum activities, which leaves him the time to look after the administrative side. At the same time he can assess more accurately what his outgoings are likely to be.

When a contractor is considering his overall costs for his own plant there are certain basic points he has to include. They are as follows:

1. Initial capital cost and residual value.
2. Interest and service charges on the investments.
3. Monetary policy, including investment, initial and annual tax allowances.
4. Maintenance and repair costs.
5. Cost of administration, insurance, licensing and legal documentation.
6. Cost of fuel and other consumable items.
7. Cost of operating and supervisory personnel.

All the above items of overheads have to be borne whether or not the work is proceeding. Therefore, the longer the machines are kept at work the lower the unit cost will be, bearing in mind that it will be necessary to have replacement machines on hand to put in the production line to keep to a minimum breakdown time.

Preventive maintenance is far cheaper than letting a machine run on until it breaks down. The repair bills are much higher under those circumstances.

Very careful thought should be given to the types of plant to purchase; this will depend on the type of work the company or organisation is contemplating. Obsolescence comes into the scheme of things. Many manufacturers change designs at least once a year and some are now considering six-monthly changes. Naturally, if a machine becomes obsolete in a short space of time the owner has less chance of recovering his capital outlay, and the residual value is much higher than it should be and therefore difficult to dispose of. This makes the machine an uneconomical proposition.

This point must be carefully watched when considering the purchase of plant. It should influence the contractor in his decision of what to purchase and what to hire and depends on a number of factors. Among those factors the predominant items are:

1. Size of contract, description and location.
2. Facilities within the company tendering for the work.
3. Type of plant—whether or not it requires skilled operatives. The latter are expensive to keep if the machine has to stand idle due to lack of continuity of work.
4. The man responsible for deciding on policy. He should be experienced in the types of plant and, if he is, he will be able to differentiate between the type of plant to purchase and the type to hire in.
5. Utilisation—a most difficult factor to regulate. There are many reasons for this, such as the purchase of unsuitable plant or change of design of contract caused by variations in the site

condition. Even though site exploration may take place prior to commencement of work, when the work has proceeded for some time conditions may alter to such an extent as to call for more or different types of machine to handle difficult conditions.

6. Unit costs. The contractor may find his plant department has a suitable machine for a particular section of the contract, but this section is so important to the progress of the whole contract that with only one machine in the fleet he feels he must not take the risk of that machine breaking down, there being no alternative for replacement. So he hires in from a firm having a fleet of similar machines, knowing they can replace at short notice in the event of an emergency. This enables him to keep to his estimated unit cost.

7. Transport—not just for removal of excavation but for carrying heavy machinery. Whether the company has its own fleet of heavy transport or not, the cost per mile run is high. With company-owned vehicles, unless they are kept employed regularly they become uneconomical due to the high cost of licensing and insurance rates. In addition, maintenance costs are heavy. With plant-hire companies becoming so numerous the trend is for them to cut transport rates to a minimum to attract business. In some instances it is known that the hire company will put a machine on site at no transport charge and; depending on lengths of hire, it may be removed from site at no charge. Heavy haulage contractors are also competitive with their rates, so that all these points must be studied when road haulage is being considered.

Profitability: the End Product

With the plant-hire industry having reached maturity in Britain, it poses a most difficult situation for the contractor. He and his management have to make decisions which are, in some instances, very much of a gamble.

When plant for a particular purpose is required to be purchased or hired, or when there is a machine in the existing fleet, certain pre-requisites must be fulfilled. Apart from the practical ones of mechanical performance and reliability, most of them concern money. Whether the company is a contracting firm, plant-hire company or manufacturer, the end product is profitability. So in the end a compromise has to be arrived at. When a piece of plant is being contemplated the facts involved can be summarised in this way. First of all, initial cost and what may be expected as a residual value.

For some time the British Government allowed investment grants which coloured the picture so that contractors were in the happy position of being assisted considerably, but at time of preparation of this book it is anticipated that the Government intends ending the investment-grant system.

Also, there is a booming market for certain types of machine in secondhand sales, so that, with the grant to ease the initial payment and no lack of demand when they consider the machine should be passed on, the contractors have one headache less.

To give an accurate picture for the benefit of the uninitiated, some of the procedures to be considered, in determining whether to purchase or hire, should be clarified.

First of all, the contractor must try to estimate what type of machinery he is prepared to purchase and to hire. Once having got that firmly fixed in his mind he must then go through the process of deciding how much he is prepared to spend on facilities for repair and maintenance. Many large contractors install depots which are little smaller than manufacturers' premises. This means tying up vast sums of money and is costly to maintain. The labour overhead charges are approaching those of the manufacturers. There are two schools of thought on this important section of the industry. One is to have facilities for complete reconditioning of the plant holding, the other to have mobile service units to carry out the everyday maintenance and servicing and to change plant at a stage when it requires complete reconditioning, so cutting down the very heavy capital outlays needed to finance fully equipped depots. There could be another approach to this controversial subject. A move is already commencing in some quarters to cut out a plant depot, except for storage. When plant is required it is obtained from hire companies, particularly so when the plant is expensive to purchase and with the possibility of its being required for the one contract only.

The majority of contractors in the UK appear to favour owning their plant, whenever possible, particularly plant which can be used universally, as opposed to hire-in plant which can be expensive, especially if there is some element of uncertainty of continuity of use.

Main Hiring Markets

The three principal markets which hire in equipment are: building and contracting companies, heavy civil engineering companies (which may embrace bulk excavations), and specialised engineering companies (massed concrete foundations, either with deep-borings or conventional piling). They all have a common denominator in that their problem is the man-hour production cost. To be able to compete in present-day industry, machines and mechanical aids have to play a major part. To be able to survive, therefore, a company must be highly mechanised and either own its own plant or be able to hire it competitively.

Regrettably, it is often the case that a man in charge of a piece of equipment that could be costing £40 000 or more has had no specific training on that machine. A most unsatisfactory state of affairs and one that points yet again to the need for operator training, and once more highlights the advantage of hiring plant and operator together. A man who has been trained and is greatly experienced in that type of equipment ensures greater productivity and less likelihood of breakdown which, no matter how speedy may be the hire company's replacement service, is to be avoided as far as possible.

It has been said with considerable justification, on many occasions in the past, that the skill of the driver is probably more important than the type of machine he drives and this factor must be taken into account when the contractor is debating whether to hire or to buy his equipment. Usually a hire driver will produce more from his own machine than any site driver who is new to it. He will work the machine with respect, be attentive to maintenance according to daily schedules and will operate with considerably less risk of machine failure and costly downtime. The benefits in that respect become obvious. Of course, the contractor has to pay his operator the rate for the job, plus bonuses and fixed on-cost. Therefore he saves nothing in hard terms of operator cost in hiring the driver with the equipment, but economics of plant operation are entirely dependent on degree of utilisation irrespective of whether the plant is purchased or hired.

Factors affecting this must include specialisation of the plant and its availability from a hire company, manufacturers' deliveries, capital availability for purchase, and facilities at the contractors' disposal for adequate maintenance. It is all a question of cost comparison of hiring over an estimated period and the equivalent cost of ownership over a similar period.

World Spread of Leasing

Although the American system of plant hire in the construction industry differs a great deal from the British method, the business world has not been slow to realise the money to be made out of what they prefer to call the 'leasing business'. Although this is not limited to leasing construction equipment, but encompasses all kinds of plant, computers, machinery and services, it does involve itself very considerably with the construction business. There are billions of dollars wrapped up in it and what originated in the USA is virtually sweeping through Europe and Japan, the developing nations of Africa, Latin America, and the Far East. This is *big* business.

Industrial equipment leasing, which in 1952 was barely a $10-million business is now nearing a $20-billion annual volume in the USA. Although major US leasing companies have been in the world market for years, concentrating mainly in Europe, equipment leasing is still attracting newcomers and expansions, with a growing list of potential customers.

First National of Boston's decision, in 1970, to go into Japan on a major scale, with Japanese partners, was indicative of the rapid expansion of lease techniques for capital equipment expansion needs in the Far East. Meanwhile, in south-east Asia, Hertz car rental company moved into heavy equipment fields, renting out heavy construction, logging and mining machinery.

Speaking in mid-1970, Ned Mundell, president of US Leasing Corporation, said that leasing in Germany had grown 50% a year over the past five years; in France it had grown 40% annually; and in Japan the growth had been 40–50%.

Lease contracts in Europe totalled $1·3 billion at the end of 1968. Stanford Research Institute have estimated that this figure will reach $15 billion by the end of 1980. In Japan, Bank of Boston's leasing venture, with $10 million on the books to start with in 1970, expected their business to double or triple in the next couple of years. Even Exim Bank prepared a plan to finance sales of US goods aimed for leasing abroad.

Manufacturers hoping to cash in on the advantages of leasing over borrowing will find many of the options available in the US, and a few extras besides in overseas deals.

TAW International Leasing, with continent-wide operations in Africa by mid-1970, had unearthed at least $14 million worth of potential business in 11 countries and expected to lease nearly $9 million worth of equipment in Africa in the ensuing 12 months.

Overseas leasing can, of course, save companies foreign exchange in establishing a new plant abroad, besides offsetting restrictive investment regulations. The lessee invests in the new plant only partially with his own funds, and leases the rest in local currency. This technique can result in a substantial reduction in foreign currency exposure. This principally affects the establishment of company property or manufacturing facilities in other countries but can also be applicable to, and influential on, the construction plant-hire business.

One of the special values to leasing overseas is as a protection against both obsolescence and inflation. In highly technological production, it is advantageous for many manufacturers to avoid tying themselves to equipment which, quickly outdated, leaves them trying to make the most of expensive but behind-the-times capital goods.

In allowing a leasing company to take the obsolescence risk, a manufacturer who leases his equipment is only bound by it for the life of the lease, typically five years. During this time the equipment user can claim his lease payments for tax relief in most countries, making up what he may have lost by the depreciation of owned equipment. Even though leasing is admittedly a costlier way of obtaining equipment than by straight borrowing, a cash flow comparison often shows that 'in the longer run leasing is cheaper than either financing or outright investment'.

A lessee can offset all his lease payments. Had he invested or borrowed, he could have depreciated the owned equipment over its useful life for tax benefits, though the US Treasury Department is reported to be considering 'cost-recovery period' depreciation which would allow firms to depreciate at more favourable individual rates, but he could have charged the lease payments in a much shorter time for a greater tax shield during those years.

If the lessee had used an accelerated depreciation schedule in countries where this is offered, depreciation allowances in later years would offer little or no tax shield, compared to the continued lease payments in the same years on non-owned equipment. Some companies use leasing as protection against inflation over the lease period. This benefits the lessee, whose payments decline in real value over time with inflation. Borrowing does not always offer the same protection against rising prices because borrowing rates may go up and contracts have their interest altered, or escalation clauses may be written into the loan repayment.

There seems to be no limit to the type of goods available on lease. Besides the usual transport equipment and machinery, there is bottle leasing in Japan and tyre leasing in Canada, and one company has even discussed leasing a yacht for exploration in the Mediterranean. In Latin America, in addition to vehicle fleets, earthmoving equipment is in heavy demand as a lease item. In Japan, Bank of Boston expects most of its business to be in $100 000–$250 000 items such as production equipment and rolling stock. Computers are not often leased in Japan now, but there is understood to be no reason why this could not also become a big item there.

In West Africa, fishing is a widespread industry and TAW plans to be ready with boats and equipment. Even leasing energy systems seems to offer vast potential overseas. Many US firms lease the heating and electrical system in their building rather than own it, and shopping centres often lease their whole power supply independently. With money like this in the leasing game, there are probably many aspects and innovations to come in plant hire for the construction industry.

Rental by the Hour

From America come reports that major dealership companies in construction equipment are shifting their emphasis from leasing under long-term financing to shorter term rentals, as a protection against future economic uncertainties. One of them, R.E. Stiegle Company of South San Francisco, California, is using a maintenance monitoring computer to devise a programme for hourly rental of heavy-duty equipment. They have purchased more than 1000 Sentry computers for installation on hydraulic cranes, excavators, air compressors and compactors. Two types of computer are available: the Sentry/7, which alerts the operator when servicing, including oil, lubrication and engine tune-up, is needed, and the Sentry/100, a more complex system that analyses six components of engine use for heavy-duty equipment.

Both systems are built around a tiny electrochemical device the size of a bean. The device, called an E-cell, can record, measure, time and monitor any event that can be translated into electrical energy.

Now, instead of renting a piece of equipment on the usual monthly basis—and typical rental for a hydraulic crane or compactor would run to $2500–$3000 per month—you can rent it by the hour.

The E-cell measures such events as engine revolutions, use-hours, operating temperature, stops and starts, and rev/min above threshhold. The customer pays on a true basis of need, while the equipment owner gets an accurate picture of equipment use which also enables him to schedule maintenance as required to prolong the life of the equipment.

In the US, the hiring industry is a thriving one, the Americans being great believers in wishing to know their working costs before they commence operations. They therefore budget on purchasing a machine, knowing that when the work is completed they will sell it for a known sum of money—they rarely keep the machine standing in their depot waiting and hoping for another job on which they can put the machine to use. Alternatively they hire, as by this method they have a fairly accurate idea of the total cost of that machine for a certain output of work. A point which may influence the choice between purchase or hire, is the part played by the elements: if the machine is owned, even though it is not working, there are standing charges to be met in the way of depreciation, but if it is hired in (and the staff are efficient) they will specify that no standing time is payable.

The basic question of making money on a construction project, no matter how large or small it may be, is very tightly geared to the choice of machine for the job and the ability of the operator to get the most out of that machine, with due regard and respect for its continued use on subsequent projects.

CHAPTER THREE

Who Hires?—Who Buys?

A controversial subject this and although there may be a pat, clinical answer, it is fair to say it is a matter of individual judgement on the part of company management to decide who hires and who buys.

The Major Factors

There are many factors to be considered, too numerous to list comprehensively, but a few of the major ones are: (*a*) economics; (*b*) quantity and condition of company fleet of plant; (*c*) type of work the company goes for and is given; (*d*) time-cycle of work—this will have a bearing on the situation when considering hire or purchase; (*e*) availability of skilled machine operators; (*f*) location of contract—distance from plant depot facilities.

Taking the six points in turn, let us try to enlarge on each one and to give a reasoned assessment.

Economics

Having been given a certain type of contract, the contractor has first of all to finally decide how and with what plant he requires to efficiently and economically carry out the work. Having decided those two points he then looks at his plant holdings. He may find that he requires much more plant than he has available in his own fleet, so then comes the decision to purchase more plant or to hire in. Now he has to look at the type of plant he requires over and above his own available fleet. If it is plant which has a universal application, then he will be tempted to purchase, but if it is specialist plant, if he is a wise contractor and provided this specialist plant is hireable, then he will hire.

Company Plant

The second point deals with the company-owned plant. Provided the contract lends itself to the plant owned by the company and provided the plant is ready and available for work, naturally the contractor will use it. There are factors which may make him hesitate. He has to assess and, knowing his future commitments, he may decide to hire in. The contract may be located three or four hundred miles from his plant base and in the locality of his contract there may be first-class facilities for hiring in plant suitable to this particular contract. If he decides to use his own plant then he must ensure that it is fully repaired and in working order and be trouble free under normal conditions for a considerable period. If the contract is large enough, he will most probably decide to have a plant workshop on site together with a stores for his mechanical and non-mechanical plant and equipment. This will require suitable staff such as a plant foreman and chief storekeeper. These must be reponsible and loyal servants of the company as they will be responsible for the efficient working of the plant. Not enough emphasis is placed on the integrating of these two employees. Most contractors employ local people in these positions, but if the wrong types get in it can lead to financial troubles and loss of machine working time—all of which holds up the work and again hits the company financially.

Preventive maintenance is essential while the plant is out on the site. If the contractor hires in plant in quantity on a particular contract he will find that hire companies are now so well organised they will install facilities and personnel on the site to ensure their machines are kept working. It is in their interests, as well as the contractor's, to have machines working and not broken down. Most contractors are now well schooled in operating plant maintenance systems.

Type of Work

Coming to the type of work, a contractor, if he is wise, will try to build up a reputation for being a specialist in some particular facet of the trade, whether building or civil engineering. Gradually, over the years, he will build up a reputation for being a fair dealer and producing a first-class job, provided he is allowed a fair remuneration for his efforts. Under reasonable conditions he will find he can make progress and he will be called upon to tender for work rather than have to go looking for it. With the policy of taking work of similar character he can standardise his plant holding. By doing so his plant staff will find it much easier to maintain the machines; this proves an economical feature as the repairs are carried out much faster and spares stocks are kept to a minimum. So many plant stores are overloaded with expensive spares which are never required and have to be sold off at very much reduced prices.

Time Factor

The time factor on a contract is a problem, particularly in the UK, where weather plays an important part. To speed up a contract due to bad weather hold-ups, it may be necessary to double up on plant allocation. Probably the plant department at base is stretched to the full and the contractor has then to fall back on the plant hirer. Planning of a contract must be thorough but even then there are many snags which occur and disorganise the routine programme.

Skilled Operators

Quite a proportion of present-day machines require skilled operators and, due to the demand and supply of these men, competition is keen. This is another consideration which has to be borne in mind when planting a large contract. The contractor has to be quite sure he has the number of trained operators required for the machines he plans to use. If he feels there is a doubt, then once again he reverts to hiring.

Location of Contract

Economy is also affected by the location of the contract site. It may be so far away from the plant base that it is a question of installing an expensive plant workshop on site. The cost, plus normal depot costs at base, may prove so uneconomical that it is cheaper to use the plant hirer in the area, who has on-the-spot servicing facilities.

The choice between hiring and buying depends entirely on the judgement of company management and there is no set school of thought. The contract has to be carefully examined from all angles; it is in the early planning stages that a contract can be organised successfully or a complete fiasco made of it. Needless to say, there are very few complete fiascos. More and more, these days, we read of contracts being completed weeks before the contractual completion date.

Types of Hire Company

To assist the formation of a plant-hire company or division a few paragraphs of suggestions are given below. Experience shows that there are probably five main systems or types of hiring organisations:

1. The small one-man, owner–operator.
2. The large plant-hire company specialising in a few types of machine or, conversely, in a full range of machinery.
3. The civil engineering contractors who have their own hire and purchase divisions.
4. The medium-sized operator who has no thoughts of any other side to his operations.
5. The plant manufacturers who, to put emphasis on their production of machines, set up a subsidiary company.

From the above list of operators one can pick and choose, pitting one against the other, and in doing so get a very competitive rate per machine. The United Kingdom CPA organisation has its members' code of procedure, together with a schedule of rates for machines and equipment, but they do not have any enforceable authority and therefore are not in a position to more than recommend the schedule of rates they publish. These can only be used as a guide to operators and in many instances are undercut.

As far as the UK is concerned, the largest group of plant-hire companies comes under (4). They are companies operating on a local area basis, as opposed to nationally, and it is possible they will cover half a dozen counties from three depots.

The plant holding will probably be in the region of £200 000, spread over the number of depots in the company. For economic return on capital, machines will be smaller in number but larger in size than those employed in localised hire. Hire periods will tend to be longer and operating hours per working week higher. Generally, rates will not be so competitive, as the availability of such machines is less. But against this must be set higher operator costs and greater overheads.

As has been pointed out earlier, there is an economic distance one can operate from a depot and this must be very carefully worked out, bearing in mind the type of machinery being built into a hire fleet. There is a school of thought which believes that until one becomes a nationally operated plant-hire company there is not sufficient scope to make large profits. It is possible that this is a correct assumption, but it is debatable. In the UK there is a very good mixture of all the types mentioned earlier, and it is significant that a number of companies have merged or been taken over to become nationally operational.

There are four departments normally in the company: plant hire; maintenance and repair; commercial and administrative; personnel, hiring and firing. All are controlled by a board of directors. Where a company uses 'operative' plant, in other words, where drivers are employed, a personnel department is essential. There is always a large wastage due to seasonal fluctuations of work and this makes it a most difficult operation to find and keep the right type of personnel and requires a great deal of tact and common sense.

A company of the size we have described in the last few paragraphs can have as many as 100 on the permanent payroll, and the annual wage bill can be £150 000. With other outgoings and depreciation the total bill can be £500 000. So as to keep in business and make a reasonable return the machines have to be kept at work up to 70% or 75% utilisation and this can only be done by having efficient methods, reliable and loyal staff and, finally, good top management. The simpler the working methods adopted, the less chance of money being poured down the drain with expensive and totally unnecessary systems.

No apology is made for repetitive reference to the fact that the UK is virtually more enlightened than the rest of the European continent about the use and potential use of plant hire in its construction industry. This is strange and does not really correspond with the impressive progress and size of projects that have been achieved by continental contractors because, in effect, what is being said is that, in the realms of plant hire, the UK contractor is further ahead, more sophisticated and better informed than his cousins across the water.

No Tax Benefits

It is a common misconception that the man who hires his plant is better served from the point of view of tax benefits, in Britain, than the contractor who is exclusively a plant owner. In fact this is just not true, although the Selective Employment Tax situation did tend to complicate things at times, being somewhat variable in application and very much a 'sometimes thing'.

Comparison of Markets

As a background of comparison, from the British contractor's point of view, it is better to look at the American market. As has already been explained, in the USA the tendency is rather one of leasing than hiring, and certainly not along the lines of the UK. Even so, comparisons are difficult for, generally speaking, contractors tend to sub-contract out various aspects of the job and this means that on the whole the American contractor is not a big plant holder. This is quite dissimilar to the situation in Britain, wherein the main contractor is frequently found to own 50%, or more, of the plant needed for the job. This means that the British contractor has a much larger capital investment in plant than the American and, therefore, he has to plan for those periods of the year when he is not able to meet the peak. It is then that he turns to plant hire.

Technical Standards

Having watched the fantastic growth rate of the British plant-hire industry from its humble beginnings, from the immediate post-war situation with its start in breaking up war-time airfields and the like, there are many people who think it very likely that the balance between owned and hired plant will in the next 10 or 15 years develop even further in favour of the plant-hire companies. If this is so, it must inevitably depend on one very important factor—that the plant-hire companies achieve the same high degree of technical standards demanded by some contractors.

Too often, in the past, plant-hire companies have evolved from men who had little claim to being plant engineers and, perhaps, had more aspiration towards being businessmen. Because of the circumstances of the time, and the condition of the British economy in the late 1940s and early 1950s, it was an encouraging situation for many opportunists. Dozens failed and were never heard of again, but equally many made the grade and established the backbone of the plant-hire industry, with a reputation for good service and fair dealing while, at the same time, making a good profit for themselves.

Specialised Plant

Modern plant is getting more complex and a contractor cannot just exist on a hire fleet consisting of excavators, compressors and mixers. The need is now for more complicated plant and, so far, the plant-hire industry has not shown any marked indication to accommodate it. For instance, a contractor wanting a batching plant will have great difficulty in obtaining one from a plant hirer. The obvious inference is that the capital wrapped up in a batching plant will not be nearly so profitable as the similar investment in, say, cranes or excavators.

To cater for such needs the plant-hire company have to make their charges for such difficult items of plant sufficiently high to cover their investment without pricing themselves out of the hire market. A difficult equity to achieve. Machines like batching plants might work and be in demand for 12 months and then stand idle for a couple of years but it does look as though the industry, if it wants to increase its share of the market, will be forced to go more and more for plants of that sort.

At the moment, specialised plant is not generally the sort of thing that is hired, other than a few exceptions like cranes or concrete pumps (Figures 3.1 and 3.2). When it comes to the giant highway

Figure 3.1. *Reinforcing the walls for an autoroute underpass approach outside Paris, using specialised wheel- and track-mounted cranes. If this were a job in the UK it is very likely that the contractor would hire in such machines just for the duration of this aspect of the project*

construction plant, such as the expensive Guntert & Zimmermann slipform pavers, or other paving trains, they have little call from the construction industry. The construction firms capable of undertaking contracts large enough to warrant the use of such machines are comparatively few in Britain and tend to be sufficiently specialised to justify their investment in plants of that nature.

In the few instances where a job requires such equipment, for short-term usage, it is not unusual for the manufacturers to hire out direct to the contractor. But this really is not true plant hire. This is

Figure 3.2. *At times there were* 10 *tower cranes, plus gantries and mobile cranes, on this site of the Parc des Princes sports stadium in Paris. The British hire system would have saved the contractor money.*

more of a private arrangement between two privately concerned parties to benefit jointly from their experience of use.

Evaluating Hire

In general, the more typical processes of evaluation and decision of what plant should be hired for a particular project start in the planning stage. Discussions take place between the contractor and the plant-hire company as to the nature of the job and what plant is going to be employed. It is common knowledge that very often firms have internal hire rates that are different (they should be lower, of course) from their external hire rates, so the first things to be decided by the contractor are: (a) what plant is already available if the contract is obtained at a certain time; (b) what is worthwhile buying to make up deficiencies in the existing plant holding; and (c) whether the required plant can be hired from an external source. It is then that the economics of the operation are presented, for now the contractor must assess with care whether it is going to be more profitable to buy a piece of plant and throw it away after a year, or hire it and pay anything up to double for its use, which is very easy to do, especially on small items like little vibrators, plate compactors, and suchlike.

All of which looks very clear-cut and simple. Anybody, it might be thought, can assess what plant is required to do the job and compare it with the equipment he has available—but all too often the state of things has changed very much from the initial planning stage to the actual state existing at the time of starting the contract.

Usually, the reason lies in the winning of another job or two in the interim which makes unexpected demands on the plant availability, because the plant originally planned for the job has been reallocated on to another contract, is being used, has broken down, has been sold, or even may have been thrown away (although the latter is unlikely). But whatever the reason, it is always a contingency that is likely to arise, and it is then that re-thinking has to begin on whether to purchase or to hire to make good the deficiencies. Of course, in such circumstances, it is always very likely that hiring will provide the best answer because it permits flexibility of operation, enabling the contractor to play 'put and take' with his machines and re-locate his plant in an integrated overall planning which may embody the needs of two or three contracts operating at the same time.

Behind every well-planned decision, however, there is always present the possibility that the machines needed may not be available from the plant-hire company and the contractor is forced to buy in even though he may prefer to hire. Take, for instance, a recent case where a contractor required a higher capacity of concrete batching than his existing plant was capable of. He was faced with the alternative of hiring another batching plant. Such machines being in short supply on the hire market and so expensive as to guarantee to the hiring company the return of their investment in twelve months, the contractor was faced with no alternative other than purchase of the plant which, after close of contract, might or might not be the idle representation of capital depreciation in his yard. Of course, there is always the other possibility that a contractor can, in turn, become a hirer out of such plant. If that happens, it must be remembered that such a contract must inevitably include the maintenance and spares replacement service that is an integral and indivisible part of the plant-hire business.

However, the example quoted was an easy, if unenviable, decision for the contractor to make because, on the one hand, he was going to outlay the same money and in one case at least have the machine at the end of the year's period, whereas on the other hand he would only have had one year's use (and the service guarantee, of course). It is not so simple with something like an excavator, a tractor or loader. In that case, more factors can be brought to bear that complicate the decision.

If the plant is in the contractor's yard there is no problem. It goes straight to work. But if it is not in stock it has to either be hired or bought (Figure 3.3). Which is going to be the cheaper? This question

Figure 3.3. *Wide selection of equipment from Germany, Japan, USA and UK in a typically well-stocked plant-hire company's yard*

is not an easy one to answer. If continual use throughout the life of the plant can be expected, working until it falls to pieces or is sold, it will probably be more profitable to buy the plant outright.

On the other hand, if there is only going to be intermittent usage it will probably be more sensible to hire from an outside source. Added to these considerations is the question of capital expenditure and cash flow. There may well be occasions when it is more desirable to spend the money, even if it is a little more costly, over a protracted period rather than pay in one lump sum in an outright purchase. It may be less expensive to pay the hire charges than either have the problem of immediate expenditure or pay interest rates on a loan. It is all a question of cash flow and availability of funds.

Under present-day conditions funds are usually very expensive to obtain either as bank loans, hire-purchase agreements or other means, and all these things have to be worked out relatively before the decision is taken. So much care must be taken, because of the cost involved, that a decision can take weeks to finalise, evaluating all the factors. On a machine like an excavator, for instance, there is no great problem because there is a well-established market rate and the contractor has a pretty good idea of his costs of operation, and potential utilisation factor and life of the machine. All of which points to the fact that, at this stage of negotiations, the construction business becomes more of an accountant's job than an engineer's job.

How Much is Hired?

Generally speaking, if one takes the total annual plant expenditure on an hourly basis by a general contractor in Britain, it is quite surprising how consistently it shows that the most equitable proportion is two-thirds purchased and one-third hired. It is very difficult to see why or how this ratio should so consistently occur, but experience certainly shows this to be so.

It is also difficult to guess what kind or size of contractor reaps the most benefit from the hiring of plant. It seems to be equally valuable to all grades of company, from the small builder to the middle-sized firm and to the real giant-sized construction corporation. They all make it work in their own sphere and in their own way. It may well be that two comparably sized firms each benefit similarly but in differing ways. What suits one does not perhaps suit another. Some companies are highly capitalised and prefer to invest in their own equipment and use it intensively. A good example of this might be a firm that tends to specialise in piling or foundation work. That sort of plant cannot be hired readily and the policy would be wrong if, as specialists, the company did not invest in equipment that could so evidently be utilised to the full. On the other hand, however, if the company is diverse in its undertakings, working on harbours, runways, highways, structures, etc., it is much more likely that it would carry considerably less investment in plant.

Some types of equipment do tend to be predominantly hired rather than purchased as a general rule. Immediately, in this category, there come to mind items like the smaller hydraulic excavators (Figure 3.4). Some contractors admit that it is difficult to see how people in their business can make these machines pay, when compared with the hire rates, although not everybody can see this. The

Figure 3.4. *Hired hydraulic excavator on a sewerage scheme where limited access required special equipment (courtesy Hydraulic Machinery Ltd.)*

excavator is one of the maids-of-all-work and there is nearly always something that can be done with the excavator's numerous attachments these days.

Free Trial

Although it is no threat to, nor is it part of, the plant-hire trade, it should perhaps be mentioned here that there is another way of getting plant for the site other than buying or hiring, and this is by free trial. It is not unusual for an agent to contact manufacturers for the loan of a machine for site trial for a month. This should be discouraged because unless the agent pays the hire rate for the machine he cannot arrive at the truth in establishing the value of the particular piece of plant for his use. Naturally, manufacturers value the user's comments on trying out a new plant but in the main they should discourage extended trial periods and say to the user 'here it is for a couple of days—try it, then buy it or send it back'. Anyone can use a piece of plant for nothing and make it pay, but he is not evaluating the machine and he is learning nothing. So the sooner the trade puts a stop to this practice the better it will be for all concerned.

Training Schemes Needed

One of the major steps for the progress of the plant-hire industry in the future, however, and one aspect in which it has been found lagging, is that of training and the establishment of bona fide recognised training schemes. And one cannot really see how much further it can go as part of the civil engineering industry without engaging itself in this. With rising costs all round, and that is without ignoring the fact that earthmoving costs have been restrained to remarkably low levels over the past ten or twenty years, this matter of training assumes ever-growing importance. A great deal has been done both by the manufacturers and the contractors to improve knowledge of handling, maintenance, and operating techniques of equipment to increase safety and achieve higher productivity. Their efforts in providing excellent training schemes, combined with those of the CITB, have done a very great deal to benefit the industry. A lot of money, thought and business acumen have been expended by those sectors of industry, and now it is time that the plant-hire companies began to pull their weight collectively. This in no way overlooks the individual, well-meaning efforts of one or two companies, but what it comes to is this: until now, designers and manufacturers, with the help of the users themselves, have improved on their technology step by step, at the same time as building up their manufacturing processes at such a rate as to keep ahead of all the other costs arising about them and, above all, in such a way as to enable contractors to keep pace with the biggest price factor of them all—labour.

We are rapidly approaching a time when the manufacturers and designers are frustrated by certain critical factors to which there seems to be no immediate alternative available. For instance, how much hope is there in the foreseeable future for increasing the capacity of scrapers? These machines, and not just they alone, must surely have reached their limit. In order to make another appreciable step towards increased capacity, higher horsepower engines are required, but to achieve any significant increase in motive power on an economical basis there has to be a reduction in capacity. Or, alternatively, an over-enlargement of body size to the extent where

Figure 3.5. 110 ton *truck-mounted crane placing escalators in Regent Street, London— a good example of where hired plant is needed for the quick short job (courtesy Richards and Wallington)*

other factors are incapable of maintaining their level of efficiency. Tyres, for instance, are a significantly weak link in this chain.

Therefore, if little more can be expected from the machines themselves, the responsibility for sustaining price control in equipment operation must devolve upon those responsible for (a) selection of the right equipment for the job, (b) scheduling and programming of the plant on site, and (c) those directly responsible for the operation of that plant—the drivers and operators. Only by full and adequate training of the operators can the best performance be obtained and the risks of downtime, due to poor day-to-day maintenance and misuse of the machines, be lessened. After all, to continue to attract the contractor, the best inducement that the hiring business has to offer is that their machines are in the hands of experts who really do know how to get the best out of them and keep the productivity figures up. This all adds up to the hire companies recognising the need to thoroughly train their personnel and to regard the cost involvement as an investment.

A recent major breakthrough in this problem has been in crane hire, however. Crane driving is a very specialised form of operation, more skilled probably than any other on site, and that is why a crane cannot be hired without its driver and why best use can be assured from hired cranes (Figure 3.5). In this respect, one crane-hire company is performing a real service to the industry of plant hire. For the first time in the industry's history we have an instance of a plant-hire company setting up a training school and issuing licences to the operators who have been through the school.

In our opinion, it is a monstrously bad thing that any man who is not properly trained should be allowed to operate so potentially dangerous and lethal piece of equipment as a mobile tower crane, or a tower crane. In British law one is compelled to be licensed to drive an invalid carriage, an electric-powered milk float, even a motorised lawn mower, and any form of motor car and yet, until now at least, there is no restriction on anyone operating a tower crane over densely populated sites and surrounding areas, where lives and property may be endangered.

In the past, the CITB has done what it could to promote training but there has been no legislation forcing companies to train their operatives or to have trained drivers, even though it is so obviously in the contractor's own interests because of the threat of litigation and the costs involved. Despite the fact that most companies recognise their liabilities and responsibilities, nevertheless the time is overdue when statutory enforcement should be applied.

The course instituted by the company mentioned is fairly extensive, lasting some 14 weeks, and at the end of it the driver is certificated as having undergone this specific course of tuition on a specified range of cranes.

Taxation and Relief

In Britain, most people are aware of the system of taxation affecting the purchase of plant, or the hire of it, but abroad there is a lot of misconception and general lack of understanding about it. So let us here establish the basic idea of how it works.

Until 1971, if a piece of plant was purchased worth £100, for example, an investment grant could be claimed equal to 20%. In addition, the normal tax allowance was granted for the life of that plant on its written down value. In other words, if it was written down over 10 years, that is £10 a year and the tax allowance that could be claimed was that claimed on the £10 a year. In addition, of course, that plant had to be maintained, which involves the purchase of spare parts and employing fitters and mechanics, and that is a normal business expenditure and obviously one that does not attract tax either. However, the investment grant scheme is no longer in effect.

There is very little difference where hired plant is concerned. All it amounts to is that all the inherent costs and expenses are bundled together in one lump sum, and are averaged out over the life of the machine. So the contractor, instead of paying out £100 in the first instance, and getting £20 back as investment grant and tax relief on the balance of £80 over a period of time, goes to the plant-hire company who has made an amalgam of all the cost involved, worked out the cost per hour to use the machine and charges it out accordingly. In that way the user does not pay tax on it. Really there is absolutely no difference or benefit to the contractor.

CHAPTER FOUR

Types of Plant and Equipment

This chapter will endeavour to define and clarify what the industry terms 'general-purpose plant and equipment' and 'specialised plant and equipment'. Some of the items will probably be controversial but, basically, general-purpose plant and equipment can be described as that appearing in the Contractors Plant Association Handbook under their rates of hire schedules. There may be a few omissions but generally speaking the machines listed are the everyday, run-of-the-mill machines coming under the heading of general-purpose plant and equipment. This is a formidable list in anyone's judgement and if a builder or contractor covers its complete range in his plant holding then he has a valuable asset, or should have. There are not many companies which can afford to have a plant holding of that size. This is another reason why the hire companies fulfil an important role in our country and why this section of the industry has grown so rapidly over the last decade.

Specialised Plant and Equipment

It is unnecessary to itemise here what we consider to be general-purpose plant and equipment; the full information may be obtained in the CPA Handbook. The more important part of this section is to try to give a representative cover of specialised plant and equipment. Quite a large proportion of this plant and equipment is designed and manufactured by the larger contracting companies and does not appear in any trade or technical publication or engineering literature. It may be seen being used on motorway construction, marine and wharf work, bridge building and tunnelling. It is therefore somewhat difficult to describe or even to name. The items of plant that come easily to mind are the specially designed cranes for placing the concrete beams and decks of elevated roads. Being in its infancy, this method of forming the roadway on concrete columns is commonly seen, but it is quite probable that the present-day methods of placing the beams and decks will be completely redesigned over the next decade.

The placing of mass concrete under water is not new but specialised equipment is necessary and can only be found in plant holdings of a small number of contractors who have specialised on marine and wharf contracts or harbour construction.

Tunnelling is contracted for by perhaps only half a dozen contractors in Britain and, again, they use very specialised tools and machinery. The present-day trend of building high-rise blocks of flats and offices has also brought in specialised plant and equipment, such as large climbing tower cranes and service hoists for personnel and goods. The hiring companies have been alert to these requirements and they have equipped themselves with these expensive and specialised machines.

In motorway construction the placing, laying and finishing of concrete or tarmacadam surfaces is carried out by specialised paver-finishers and slipform machines working to very fine limits.

Large earthmoving machinery is also becoming specialised. The electric-powered wheel scrapers, with multi-scraper loader assistance, are designed to speed up the time spent in filling the scraper bowl. These machines are powered fore and aft with 750 hp turbo-charged diesel engines. The large 75–100 ton carrying capacity dumptrucks and overburden-stripping excavators with high-capacity buckets, come under the heading of specialised plant. In the heavy-lifting section of the industry, cranes capable of handling 165 tons are with us and the modern trend is to have a telescopic boom hydraulically operated from the driver's cab to speed up the time of crane arriving on site to starting the work of lifting. Even the spuds for supporting the crane when lifting are hydraulically operated from the driver's cab. This is another side of the industry catered for by the plant-hiring companies. Water-control equipment in the form of de-watering plant may also be described as specialised plant and equipment. A number of contractors have their own plant but at present it is not universally used. There is still a faction adopting the old method of using a series of pumps dotted all over the site, which are merely pumping water from one place to another. Many contractors fight shy of using a dewatering plant, presumably because they consider it too much trouble and possibly expensive to install. In fact, the plant is simple to install and the end result is a dry site for the duration of the contract, which outweighs the first cost of installation.

There are many more items that could be listed under specialised plant and some will be detailed further on, by reference to previous chapters and the question of buying or hiring. It has been mentioned that some of the specialised plant and equipment can be hired, but only in certain types of machinery. We would say that the majority of specialised plant and equipment items can only be purchased on a once-off basis and in many instances it is a closely guarded design of one particular contractor. Probably it will not be protected by patent but woe betide anyone caught copying the machine or equipment—a great amount of capital is expended in designing and producing these specialised machines.

Motorway Plant

The motorway programme in the UK has demanded specialist plant and equipment to a larger degree than any other type of civil engineering project. Commencing with the initial stages of a project, excavation, building and levelling is still carried out by more or less standardised plant, such as excavators, motor scrapers and graders. At the foundation of a road, where graded rock and stone were used until the last decade, low water-content, dry lean concrete is now put down and compacted. The reinforcement is then laid on top and a further layer of semi-dry lean concrete is put down and this time spreaders and finishers are used. The slipform paver, as a specialist piece of machinery, is now familiar in Britain and can still be classified as a specialist piece of machinery due to the delicacy and sophistication of mechanism operating the equipment. The final top dressings of a road are still applied in the conventional manner and do not call for specialised machinery. Where a roadway is elevated on concrete pillars, it is constructed using prefabricated beams and slabs. Placing cranes, or launching gantries, which move longitudinally with the progress of the work have had to be designed and made to handle the prefabricated units. These are very definitely specialised machines, designed and constructed by the mechanical engineering departments of civil engineering contractors.

Tunnelling Equipment

Tunnelling is another form of specialist occupation calling for mainly conventional machines but recently the digging of the tunnel shape has been revolutionised by specialist cutting equipment.

The world-wide increase in traffic density imposes restrictions on contractors working on sewers in urban areas. Now a British company has introduced a 'mini tunnel' for sewers of 900–1300 mm (3 ft to 4 ft 3 in) diameter, claiming to make tunnelling a viable proposition at depths as shallow as 3 m (10 ft).

The same company pioneered pipe jacking in Britain in the last decade but the system flagged because of the expensive temporary thrust walls, the high stress forces imposed and the large pits required. Experience gained has led to the development and successful application of the Seerflex Mini Tunnel system which is shield driven, giving effective ground support and safety to the miner and, because it is face built, eliminating problems of soil friction involved with thrusting methods. It uses only three concrete segments, not requiring bolts and erection frames, which contributes to accurate alignment. Access pits are only manhole size and the concrete segments store compactly at pit top. A light crane, big enough to lift the muck skip, is all that is needed to handle materials in and out.

Cranes

Elsewhere in this chapter it is explained that most contractors tend to purchase their specialist equipment, such as slipformers and concrete trains, as opposed to hiring them, but in the case of cranes in the larger and more specialised ranges the converse appears to be true. Equipment like, for example, a Lorrain Moto-Tower or a Gottwald are virtually unknown as pieces of owned plant. This may all be part of the way in which plant hire has grown in Britain. Plant has been available for hire and as the industry has grown the plant which it has offered for hire has grown with it, enhanced by the development of a strong and viable plant-hire industry. All of which makes good sense economically, but it is like the chicken and egg riddle: do contractors hire the equipment because the industry is there—or is the industry there because people will hire?

Why hire a crane? If this question is asked, surely the answer must be because of the need for mechanisation to meet ever-spiralling labour costs? And cranes probably are the best example of the real need to use the right equipment for the job in hand to obtain efficiency from a machine. Because of the variety of jobs for lifting equipment on a building site there is a wide choice of machines to do them in the most efficient way. There is absolutely no point in using a 50 ton crane when a 6 ton one will do, or vice versa. When a range of mobile cranes between 6 and 165 tons is available to an industry it makes no sense for contractors to own just a few cranes of their own, for they are always going to be using those cranes to some extent under capacity and therefore wasting the cost involved. If a company elects to have a 20 or 40 ton crane, it will be using the 40 ton one for 30 ton jobs, and when the need arises for something in excess of 40 tons they will have nothing suitable. Maximum utilisation is essential. You have *got* to use the right machine for the job, otherwise the outlay on the machine is being wasted.

This all points to the hiring business again, whereby exactly the right machine can be used to lift the job and on the precise day it is needed. The right machine at the right time doing the right job. That is what contract efficiency consists of. No contracting company could hope to obtain maximum utilisation from their own machines over a range so wide as the 6–160 ton mobile, truck-mounted machines that can be obtained from just one hire company, to say nothing of the other crane hirers in the business. If the contractor has a wide enough range of his own machines to ensure that he is not either under- or over-using capacity, then he cannot expect to get the 80% utilisation factor which guarantees efficiency. You cannot have it both ways.

Cranes tend to fall within a specialised field of equipment for consideration but the arguments that are applicable to them are equally valid for several other pieces of contractors' and builders' plant. Every company, of course, must ultimately be responsible for making its own evaluation of the economics on which the decision whether to hire or buy stands. It has to determine the degree of utilisation but, in the case of crane use, the whole thing is much more clearly defined and the decision is not so difficult as with some other pieces of plant. It is not difficult to see that to recoup the £50 000 or so that, for example, a 50 ton Lorrain costs to buy, the owners have to get about 80% utilisation. And very few building firms can see their employment sufficiently far ahead to predict that degree of utilisation with certainty.

Hoists

More and more builders and contractors are becoming used to considering hoists wherever men and materials have to be elevated on structural work. Before discussing types and benefits of hoists, it is sequentially preferable to consider the reasons for using a hoist at all. In fact this is a part of building that has been the subject of a great deal of research in many countries, particularly in Germany and Scandinavia.

According to German investigation, a contractor who does not

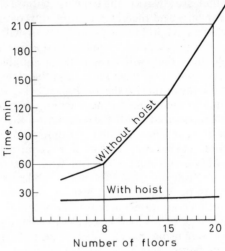

Figure 4.1. *Time lost climbing without hoist*

use a hoist, will lose one hour per worker per day on a total of four single trips up to 8th floor level. An additional 10 min must be added per worker, day and floor for work carried out between the 9th and 15th floors. When working on and above the 16th floor, 15 min must be added per worker, day and floor.

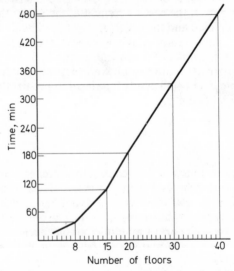

Figure 4.2. *Time gained per worker-day by using hoist*

Swedish research has shown that the time taken to walk to and from the hoist, together with possible waiting time and the time required to walk from the hoist to the actual work place, has been assessed at about 4 min. This is based upon a hoist speed of 0·65 m/sec, with a distance between floors of 3 m. To simplify the comparison, each worker is presumed to make four single trips per day.

Figures 4.1 to 4.3 indicate clearly the outcome of these researches.

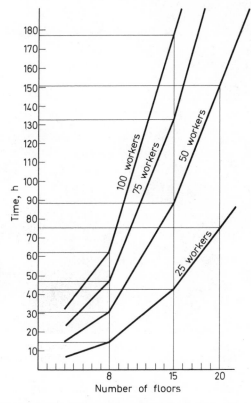

Figure 4.3. *Time gained in hours per day when using hoist on sites with* 25, 50, 75 *and* 100 *workers*

The two types of hoist mainly used for building and construction are dependent either on wire-rope operation or on rack and pinion (Figures 4.4 and 4.5). The Swedes have tended to favour the latter system and it has found considerable popularity in Britain. The manufacturers claim the system can cut erection times and direct labour costs by as much as 80% on construction sites, and can be

Figure 4.4. *Inside the Drax Power Station chimney, working with an Alimak rack-and-pinion hoist. The chimney was built to a height of 260 m (850 ft) (courtesy 600 Group)*

used with complete safety for carrying passengers and goods at heights up to 30 m (100 ft). The hoist can be quickly and easily erected on site, the first 30 m being erected in one day without site cranage. The rack-and-pinion system eliminates ropes and the drive gear uses twin motors, worm gearboxes and double climbing pinions. Three metre (10 ft) mast extensions can be added in 20 min and the mast sections and landing gates are pre-wired, obviating the need for a skilled electrician, so no site wiring is necessary other than connection to the mains supply.

These hoists are well suited for slip-form construction and the

Figure 4.5. *External view of the Drax Power Station chimney, the largest ever built in Western Europe. It has a diameter of 26 m (86 ft), at ground level, and is built to a height of 260 m (850 ft). The project was completed in about 2½ years, during which time each hoist cage travelled a distance of approximately 2000 miles (courtesy 600 Group)*

pinions which climb the hoist are spring loaded for even-tooth loading on the climbing rack. During erection, dismantling and operation, the cages are always locked to the mast and a patented safety gear is centrifugally operated and positively driven by a pinion which is permanently engaged with the climbing rack.

Another recently introduced hoist is a high-speed system which can quickly transport men and materials up and down towers, chimneys, buildings, and similar tall structures, some two and a half times faster than the standard hoist. This is economical at heights in excess of 60 m (200 ft). Another type of Swedish hoisting system, intended for low- and medium-rise buildings, is self-erecting and portable. It is hydraulically operated to make the raising machinery lighter and more efficient. For transportation purposes the length of the mast section has been kept to minimum dimensions by designing the mast to fold in two sections. This new hoisting system can be erected to a height of 13 m (42 ft) in under 3 min and will carry 8 passengers or 660 kg (1450 lb) of materials. Further mast sections may be added to reach to a maximum height of 30 m (100 ft).

Makers of rack-and-pinion hoist systems claim that British building contractors are reluctant to use a conventional wire-rope hoist on a block of flats below eight floors, for the cost of initial erection varies between £300 and £500, and the time factor is anything up to a week. They offer, by comparison, erection of their hoisting system for, say, a four-floor block, which takes a matter of minutes and the cost can be measured in pence, making it the ideal equipment for low-rise construction sites. A further advantage is that the machine can be quickly towed around the site with the hoist raised to a landing height of 13 m (42 ft).

An example of the economics of these hoists concerns one which the contractor bought for £8794 and was repurchased by the distributor after two years and resold for £6000. The recovery was therefore 68·33% of purchase price. Looking at this particular transaction another way, the figures indicate the cost of owning a hoist was £2794 over 82 weeks which equals £34.07 per week. This makes the cost per cage £17.03½ per week, which is less than the hire rate for a conventional goods hoist.

Naturally, manufacturers of wire-rope hoists dispute the claims of their competitors and do not agree that there is a reluctance among British contractors to use the conventional wire-rope operated equipment.

Makers of wire-rope hoists claim their system is still the safest, cheapest and most efficient means of raising and lowering the cage. To extend working heights the problem has been that in many instances during an extension the rope had to be released and re-reeved over the pulleys. Even on hoists where some thought had been given to extension technique so that re-reeving was unnecessary, the wire rope still had to be unloaded when surplus rope was paid off the winding drum to cater for the extended height.

Wire rope becomes a nuisance when it is unloaded; the coils on the winding drum tend to unravel due to the natural spring of the wire, the rope may become displaced from the pulleys, and kinks can develop along its length. All these possibilities have to be checked and rectified before tension is reimposed, which is an arduous and time-consuming operation. As a result, one manufacturer has devised a method of constant-tension spooling, whereby the wire rope is taken from the winding drum, over a fixed pulley some $3\frac{1}{2}$ m (12 ft) above the base, then under a pulley attached to a sliding carriage, up and over the sliding cathead and finally down to the cage where it is attached. When extending a hoist the cage is driven up, and locked to the mast. The hoist down control is operated so that the winding drum pays off rope.

The manufacturer offers a range of three items utilising this system, covering a single-cage materials and passenger hoist, and a twin-cage model as well as a dual-purpose materials and passenger hoist and concrete elevating skip. These have a payload quoted as 1016 kg (1 ton) or 12 men per cage and 480 litre ($\frac{5}{8}$ yd³) for the concrete skip, operating at 0·686 m/s (135 ft/min).

Makers say that for the most part the tendency is for hoists to be bought outright by contractors and not so often by plant-hire firms, but taking for example a twin-cage hoist operating to a top landing height of 61 m (200 ft), this sort of machine at current prices would cost about £8374. Assuming a continuous hire of 78 weeks (a reasonable write-off period for this equipment), this would have to work out at about £107 per week. Incidentally, the Federation of Civil Engineering Contractors' Handbook schedule of hire rates, applied to contractors' own plant, quotes £2.03/h for a 30 cwt /18 men cage hoist, which seems to be the nearest comparison published at this time.

Specialist Companies

Increasingly in Britain we are witnessing the evolution of hire companies that specialise in the equipment they handle. Firms tend to limit the type of equipment (sometimes even the makes of equipment) that they offer for hire, so that they become absolute specialists in that particular line. The advantages are readily apparent. It facilitates spares stocking, tooling, and expertise in maintenance and operation. In many cases it enables the hire companies to serve in the role of consultants to a project and certainly be more than plant owners renting out their equipment devoid of anything other than profit on the machine.

This is probably more apparent in the business of hiring cranes than any other, particularly mobile cranes. Generally these have a pricing that can be calculated at a rate of £1000 per ton lift capacity. In other words, a 10 ton capacity crane will cost about £10 000 for a lattice-girder jib, self-propelled mobile crane, but hydraulic jib models are more expensive and there is no similar basis for calculation, which means that the companies hiring them out are really specialists and deal exclusively in that type of equipment.

The term 'plant hire' is not by any means universal. It does not have the same connotation in any other part of the world as it does in the UK. What the Germans often seem to know as plant hire is really what is termed contract earthmoving in Britain, and it would interest German contractors to learn that in Britain there are companies, such as one crane-hire firm, who augment their activities as a major plant-hire firm by having a subsidiary company which undertakes contract earthmoving work. In fact, at times they may even go a step further and establish a construction company as well. This contract earthmoving company is an entirely autonomous operation which owns its own plant fleet of scrapers, loaders, etc., but if additional equipment is needed then this can be hired from the parent company. It is yet another manifestation of the flexibility and advantages of the British system. In addition, this firm while owning more than 1000 machines is additionally involved in the actual selling of such machines. This is yet another offshoot done through another of their companies, which also sells and hires cranes of manufactures other than their own. All this evolves from the business of crane hire.

Consider a machine such as the 165 ton Gottwald, until recently the largest mobile crane in UK, with 17 gears and 28 wheels which travels on highway under its own power and costs about £170 000 to buy (Figure 4.6). This is really specialised equipment and for such a piece of plant special hire terms apply, of course. It is no small operation just getting this three-man machine to site. It is an on-highway machine, totally road-going, but in most cases an all-in charge is made for the job to allow for the costs involved in transportation to and from the site; so this means that it would be impractical to quote a per day price and it is more usual for the job to be priced, not the machine. In fact, the price is really based on a three-part tariff consisting of one rate for travelling time, another rate for erection time and a third rate for working time. Taking a hypothetical example, if this machine were hired for a three-week job the hire charge would probably exceed £5000—and that is certainly less than a period of ownership, with less than maximum utilisation, would cost.

But here again, with this type of equipment there arises the additional benefits of hire, because the concept extends much further than just using the machine. Because of the size of the Gottwald it gets involved in very big jobs, lifting in one piece things that no other machine could. Therefore the machine is called in when, for example, things like flare stacks or similar have to be lifted in one piece when there is no other means of doing the job. These are big

Figure 4.6. 165 ton *Gottwald tower crane placing tubular steel section on factory site (courtesy Richards and Wallington)*

complicated jobs and the hire company comes into it with consultancy and advice for the contractors involved in that part of the lifting operation, so that the whole plan of erection can be properly organised around what the machine can do, and the entire plant hire really becomes a contract operation.

The hire company does in effect become so involved as to be part of the critical path planning, fully consultative, having been brought into the picture so that they advise the client in matters of off-loading and stacking of materials and positioning around site. Even the order of scheduling other aspects of the work so as to get the most economical use from available cranage and to minimise time involved in hiring the big machine are included. This even extends to their making suggestions as to other aspects of plant utilisation on site with regard to the complete sequence of lifting operations. This is a proper and full planning service, saving the customer money.

Plant Hire and Merchanting

The successful plant-hiring companies in the UK have specialised on the type of plant and equipment they are geared to understand and can accommodate in their organisation. There are still hire companies who endeavour to combine plant hire and merchanting and in quite a number of instances make a success, but there are others who have dropped one or the other, usually the merchanting side. The problem with combining the two is the labour force required to maintain the hire fleet and to handle repair work on the merchanting side. Therefore, a company must look very carefully at its position and decide on the following circumstances: (*a*) whether to combine the two sections of business; (*b*) the type and capacities of plant holding—specialisation or a large range of plant; (*c*) whether to concentrate their activities in one area or become a national organisation.

Specialisation can be arrived at in two ways—by trade or machine. Some companies prefer it by trade and by this method it is allied to a number of sections in the contracting and civil engineering professions. A few examples are road building, quarrying, opencast coal mining, bulk earthmoving, marine works and tunnelling. All these facets of the industry command a range of specialised plant (Figure 4.7). To illustrate the situation in the UK at present, the specialist plant-hire holdings are valued at £80m with 30% of this figure invested in cranes of all types and sizes.

The next largest holding is heavy earthmoving plant with the motorised scraper being the predominating units of plant. Another aspect of specialised plant is that for the supply and placing of concrete. With the advent of the ready-mixed truck vehicle, concrete is being prepared and mixed at centralised points, then loaded into a lorry-mounted agitator which keeps the mix at the correct consistency during the period of transportation and prevents

Figure 4.7. *Bulldozing to maintain haul road for fast earthmoving on a motorway contract. Hired plant was used to augment contractor-owned fleet to avoid depletion of work-force on other sites (courtesy Richard Costain Ltd.)*

segregation. Where there is no central mixing point, only bulk storage, it is necessary to use a truck mixer which can operate at greater distances from base.

Coming to the question of what is considered to be specialist plant, we have mentioned that the everyday type of plant is dealt with by the handbook produced by the Contractors Plant Association of Great Britain. Specialised plant consists of 'one-off' machines designed by the contractor, and that can be cranage, concrete placing, bulk storage of materials; large overburden stripping machines which have no other application; tunnelling machinery, which again has no other application, and service and personnel lifts for high-rise building blocks (Figure 4.8). There are many other machines and pieces of equipment too numerous to list, but a broad picture has been set out.

When a contractor is purchasing plant or equipment he has in mind two factors: that it will assist him in getting his work done quickly and more efficiently, and that it will cut working costs and so influence his profitability. The fact that on a motorised unit the power shift system incorporates an oil-cooled, modulated engine clutch positioned ahead of the single-stage torque converter, which transfers power through the power train to the previously engaged transmission clutch pack, does not really interest him nor may he desire to own such a machine. His main concerns are—how much earth will it shift in the shortest time; how much maintenance does it require; what interval of time is there between major overhauls and, an important question, what after-sales service is available.

Manufacturers of plant are convinced they supply their customers with the machines they require, but they are very prone to making modifications which render the previous machine obsolete. We have seen exhibitions organised and fade away. One reason is that purchasers of plant are weary of seeing machines to all intents and

Figure 4.8. *Double use from this rope-operated hoist for passengers and concrete placing. Note chute and hopper (courtesy Wickham Engineering Co. Ltd.)*

purposes the same as they were 12 months before, but which have had only some slight modification carried out. Alternatively, they may have been motivated by competition to vary a range, which might not be entirely in the contractor's interests.

Earthmoving Problems

Excavation of earth, particularly where it is virgin ground, always poses problems. Prior surveys are vitally necessary but even then contractors have been financially embarrassed by encountering strata faults which have not been brought to light during the survey. Apart from the freak occurrences which have to be overcome, there is some new thinking among bulk earthmoving contractors and more scientific know-how being employed. The immediate proposals are limited to improving the cutting edge of the machine and its mode of attacking soil, and a reallocation of power to the machine components. Looking further ahead, there will have to be a fundamental change in the approach to excavation. Manufacturers tend to pin their designs to brute force. We now have the coupling of two motor scrapers to achieve a larger tonnage shifted in a shorter time, but at what an expense? In the hands of any but really skilled drivers the cost per unit measurement can be astronomical, apart from cost of maintenance and repairs to the plant and tyre wear and replacement. Correctly operated, however, the system can pay handsome dividends.

The logical approach to dealing with bulk excavation on a more modern concept must be directed to the earth-to-soil relationship. To bring about a change in the physical characteristics and strength of the soil to be cut, rather than to increase the power required for the machine. By drilling the perimeter of excavations and using the old and well-tried methods of the quarrying industry, and disturbing the boundaries of the excavation, it enables the machine to bite more easily into the bulk and so reduce the initial power required. Gases can be expanded in a cylinder and the resultant forces transmitted to the digging element by complicated mechanisms. Another method would be to inject and expand the fuel into the soil itself, via the teeth on the machine bucket. It has been proved by geologists that nature removes whole continents by this process.

Vibratory Techniques

Another alternative approach is to make use of vibratory techniques. Investigations have shown the feasibility and advantages of passing power to a hammer head by hydraulic wave motion. By achieving resonance between the waves and the soil, this system can be applied in drilling or piling hammers. For earthmoving requirements reduction of resistance in some soils may be achieved by projecting a wave motion forward of the tool into the soil.

Expansion of Capacity

To keep pace with the demand for water, food and services the construction industry will have to increase its capacity in relation to the world gross product. Examination of the overall demand indicates that road construction and the building of water conservation projects will both expand at above the average rate. By the end of the next five years industrial countries will be spending something in the region of 40% more than they did in 1965. Developing countries will treble their road construction expenditure. In the UK, water requirements are expected to increase fourfold over the next two decades, calling for a large-scale programme of water conservation construction schemes.

Population growth in the urban areas of the world will have a particular effect on the construction industry—it is expected that city and town dwellers will increase on a world basis by nearly 50% in the next decade. This one zone of development has already created markets for new models and types of machine, such as the backhoe mounted on the hydraulically operated tractor/excavator. Another fast-growing market is that of heavy-duty highway trucks to move materials from the urban development site.

Looking ahead on a broad basis, the pattern is, therefore, one of great expansion. As the world demand increases, the number of manufacturers of plant, the number of different models of machine available, and the number of customers are expected to become less complex. There will be fewer manufacturing organisations, fewer product models, with more discerning customers. This trend is well under way in the UK and in Europe and America.

Two years ago there were, in the UK, in excess of 400 acquisitions and mergers by over 300 companies, for an expenditure of approximately £1600m. Already, forces are at work reducing the complexity in the number of organisations producing construction equipment. As competition increases this trend will gather momentum. The plant-hire industry in this country is also going through the stages of crystallisation and there are signs that the major volume of plant hire available on a national basis could be undertaken in the next decade by four or five organisations.

In the year 2000

In the USA today, 60% of the industrial assets are already owned by 200 enterprises and it is predicted that 60% of the world's business will be conducted by 200 companies by the year 2000. As manufacturers merge, there will be fewer models and types of construction plant and equipment. This aspect of the development of the industry is only just taking place. Currently there is a swing towards a proliferation of equipment types. Most of these can be attributable to fringe manufacturers attempting to keep away from the main demand areas which are quickly becoming tough competitive fields of the large-volume producers. Examples of fringe products are displayed each year at the large European trade fairs. Many have a brief production run and rarely enjoy more than local markets.

As volumes increase and as the smaller manufacturers leave the field, or merge, there will be more objective assessment of what the

Figure 4.9. *Largest and smallest of a range of crawler tractors. The smaller has 59 maximum engine horsepower and weighs 4780 kg (10 538 lb). The other, claimed to be the world's largest, has 524 net flywheel horsepower with a bare shipping weight of 46 039 kg (101 500 lb) (courtesy Allis-Chalmers Corporation)*

Figure 4.10. *Loaders at work in a quarry, excavating limestone from the face and keeping a shuttle fleet of 16/19 yd³ rear dumps busy (courtesy International Harvester Co. of Great Britain Ltd.)*

construction industry is basically trying to do and the plant required to do it.

The main volume-demand areas are already clearly defined. The four most popular types of machine on a world-volume basis are the crawler tractor (Figure 4.9), produced at the rate of approximately 65 000 machines per annum, the industrial wheeled tractor, at approximately 62 000 units, the hydraulic excavator, at approximately 25 000 units, and the four-wheel-drive loading shovel (Figure 4.10), at approximately 20 000. These four types of machine represent about 80% of the total world unit volume—an industry with a current turnover exceeding £2500m per annum. The commercial application of these types of machine is relatively short in years.

Ranges Widened

Major manufacturers have also, at the same time, widened their range. One American company, for example, based their business

Figure 4.11. *Bulldozer pushloading a conventional scraper, while an elevating scraper works alongside unaided (courtesy Clark Equipment)*

initially on crawler tractors but in the last decade have developed a full range of high-speed motor scrapers, wheel-loading shovels from 80 to 500 hp and off-highway trucks with load capacities up to 100 tons. Similarly, another company entered the market with four-wheel-drive loading shovels and now offers a range of dumptrucks, motor scrapers and hydraulic full-circle excavators. This allows the manufacturer to introduce greater scope in the production of basic assemblies such as engines, transmissions and hydraulic systems. Many of these assemblies can be common to several different models and types of machine in their range.

The plant user today has a fully comprehensive service available to him, which permits machine evaluation and profitability to be established on a machine life basis. The initial cost of the machine, although it may be well into five figures, is not the only consideration. More important is the evaluated total cost—initial cost plus overhead and operating costs less residual value. American dealers already operate total bid methods of selling machines. Few UK companies operate such schemes, but guaranteed buy-back agreements are becoming more common.

To keep pace with the growing demand for more efficient and more productive plant, the construction equipment industry has spent vast sums of money and time on basic research and development.

New development has increased dramatically over the last five years. Motor scrapers have increased in size and power from 18 yd^3 to 40–50 yd^3; in addition, a system of self-loading elevators has been incorporated to assist the time-cycles by loading much quicker (Figure 4.11). Hydraulics has become a universal development. Dumptrucks have grown from 10–15 tons to 100 tons.

The future holds great promise of new machines and fresh concepts in earthmoving. As mentioned earlier in this chapter, a new approach is being made in relation to soil displacement. A new development, named the Redsod development, is a 'repetitive explosive device for soil displacement'. Energy is generated within a combustion chamber by the combustion of compressed air and a hydrocarbon fuel to displace and move soil or material. Tests with a tractor equipped with prototype dozer blade shows that a mile-long trench 10 ft wide and 5 ft deep can be opened up in 1 h by this method. Army engineers mounted a large combustion chamber between a special dozer blade and the tractor. As the cutting edge of the blade crowds into the soil, air under pressure is pumped into the chamber and fuel spray injected into it. An electric current, through a spark plug, ignites the mixture and the expanded gases are emitted with explosive force through valves and louvres in the toe of the blade. By this method the soil is disrupted and pushed to both sides through ducts. This development is primarily for the armed forces to meet requirements for high-speed trench digging. Some modified form of this new development may eventually be incorporated into civilian-use machines.

CHAPTER FIVE

Plant for the Job

Some items of equipment tend to be more specialised than machines like excavators, dumpers, small mobile cranes and site material transport vehicles. Yet despite this they are widely used, at some time or another, on sites of all kinds by builders, contractors, local authorities and civil engineers of all magnitudes. Although seemingly paradoxical it can be said that these specialised techniques are general and universal in their application. Subjects like concrete placing, dewatering and hoists are all frequently encountered on sites and although there is not space in this book to do more than select one or two examples from the many, it is to be hoped that the examples chosen may assist the understanding of, and open avenues of thought on, the manner of approach to the examination of plant usage on site and so improve knowledge of costing. If this end is achieved then it both justifies the inclusion of the few and the exclusion of the many and, in the final analysis, will assist in the decision of whether it is more profitable to hire or to buy new when the contractor is faced with the application of such techniques on a job.

Concrete Pumps and Pumping

Pumping concrete and the equipment involved are specialised businesses and it is sometimes preferable for contractors to work with a specialist sub-contractor for this work. For the most part, the conditions of access tend to govern the use of concrete-pumping methods, compared with a common alternative of placing with skip and crane. Obviously it is cheaper to pump than to utilise a crane for this job, providing there is other work for the crane to be doing on site. Tunnels, subways and overpasses are typical examples

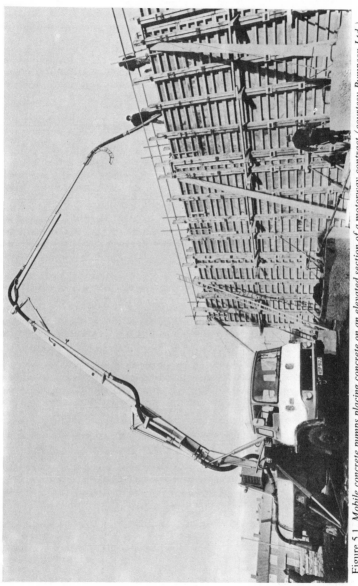

Figure 5.1. *Mobile concrete pumps placing concrete on an elevated section of a motorway contract (courtesy Pumpcon Ltd.)*

of jobs particularly suited to pumping—in fact, anywhere there is difficulty of overhead access—but almost any contract lends itself to the technique. Because of the specialised nature of this aspect of construction, and the very wide field of application in building and civil engineering, particular emphasis and space is given in this book.

In Britain, concrete-pumping equipment is generally hired rather than bought. This is because of its specialised nature and because it is so dependent on the type of concrete to be poured. The concrete is critical in the process and quality control must be exercised. Furthermore, cleanliness is essential and there is always the danger that the contractor's labourer may not be sufficiently careful in this respect; therefore it is usually safer to leave it to the specialist.

Most concrete pumping is carried out by these specialist firms who hire out equipment and trained operators to the industry and relieve the contractor of the need for investment in costly equipment and technical staff. Many of the larger contractors have their own concrete pumps, but they still rely to a large extent on pumping specialists to supplement their pumping requirements. Others, however, prefer to hire the pumps and the operators with them.

The present percentage of concrete pumped in Britain is about 3–4%. This compares with 25–30% in countries such as West Germany, Japan, the United States and Belgium, where the use of mobile small-line concrete pumps has been recognised as the most economical method for placing concrete for some years now. During the course of the next few years a tremendous expansion can be expected in concrete pumping in the UK, similar to that involving the use of ready mixed concrete some 15 years ago.

One of the largest concrete-pumping operations ever undertaken in Britain took place at the close of 1970 on a large motorway contract in Kent (Figure 5.1). The operation was a bridge deck and the volume of concrete involved was some 1070 m³ (1400 yd³). Three mobile 740C concrete pumps were placed on the job by the specialist sub-contractors and the bulk of the concrete was placed in 20 h. This gives some indication of the efficiency and time-saving potential of concrete pumps when utilised on large pours. Similar benefits are obvious on much smaller pours. Many contracts are undertaken to pump say 19·5 m³ (25 yd³) into a first-floor slab, and in the majority of cases the concrete is pumped into place and levelled in under 2 h.

Types and Selection

Time and cost are the two major factors to be considered when selecting the method of concrete placing to be used on any project.

Concrete pumps come into two basic categories, those which are piston operated and those which are on the 'squeeze' principle. Which is the more suitable is determined by the nature of the job. Of course, concrete placing using crane and skip is effective whenever there is sufficient room for access but it is not always economic— especially if it involves using a crane that could be more gainfully employed elsewhere on site. Generally speaking, a mobile concrete pump is usually the most efficient and economic method of placing concrete on a building site. It does not have the high costs of static plant, and with it a small concrete gang can place large quantities in a working day. On an interchange highway bridge in England the contractors broke two records when, in a continuous 35 h, they placed 1402 m³ of concrete on the deck. On that job the placing of 571 m³ by one of the pumps was claimed as a record pour for a single pump. Concrete was delivered ready mixed by a fleet of six truck mixers. There were four Schwing hydraulic pumps on site; a TCP 50 KVM lorry-mounted luffing boom pump with a maximum output of 45 m³/h; a BPA 24/30 KVM trailer-mounted luffing boom pump; a BPA 24/30 DVM trailer-mounted pump with lattice boom, and a BPA 24/30 DVM self-propelled with lattice boom, each having a maximum output of 30 m³/h.

Pumping was carried out initially by the three smaller pumps but was subsequently reduced to the two luffing boom machines during the day, while the third pump was reintroduced during the final stages. A fourth pump was available in the event of a breakdown but was not needed. The 1524 m (5000 lin ft) of 0·76 m (2 ft 6 in) diameter void formers, and 366 m (12 000 lin ft) of cable sheathing, made the placing of concrete extremely difficult and, though the programmed rate of 38·225 m³ (50 yd³) per hour was attained, the pumps could not be used at full capacity.

Pump Operation

The pump selected for a particular pour will be capable of pumping the quantity required over the required distance within the available time. Pumps are rated for output and delivery distance, but the actual output and distance achieved will depend on concrete pumpability and supply and on placing efficiency.

The ratio between maximum horizontal and maximum vertical distances that can be pumped will vary according to the particular circumstances, but generally ratios between 3 to 1 and 4 to 1 (horizontal to vertical) are acceptable. The maximum range is reduced due to extra drag and resistance by bends and flexible hoses.

A 90° bend is the equivalent of reducing the potential distance by about 12·5 m (41 ft).

Whenever possible the straightest path between the pump and delivery point should be taken and the flexible placing hose at the end of the pipeline should be moved in such a way as to avoid obstruction to concrete flow. The hose should never be kinked as this can cause a serious accident if pumping is allowed to continue, due to an excessive pressure build up.

Placing techniques should follow good pumping techniques; whenever possible, placing should commence at the point furthest from the pump, and pipelines should be progressively 'broken back'.

The economical use of the placing equipment depends to a great deal on the choice of diameter of the pipeline. Large diameter pipes are considerably heavier and their handling is difficult and costly. The diameter is determined by (a) size and type of concrete pump, (b) horizontal and vertical placing distances, (c) quality of concrete with regard to consistency, and (d) maximum size of aggregates.

Self-propelled and trailer concrete pumps are normally equipped with a 102 mm (4 in) or 76 mm (3 in) pipeline. With such pumps ready mixed concrete is mostly used and they often work on several building sites in one day. Placing distances are relatively short. To make their application as rational as possible, it is important to lay the pipeline as quickly and easily as possible.

Small-line pumps are those employing a 76·2mm (3 in) or 101·6mm (4 in) pipes. These sizes were adopted to facilitate handling.

The piston pumps operate by the use of dual hydraulically powered cylinders, concrete being drawn from the hopper into one cylinder on the suction stroke, whilst concrete is discharged simultaneously up the pipeline on the pressure stroke of the second piston. Valve action has to be carefully designed for smooth, even flow. 'Squeeze' pumps operate by progressively squeezing concrete out of a rubber tube, the present models using rotating rollers operating in a vacuum chamber.

Probably 90% of pumps in current use in the UK fall into the former category.

Hydraulically operated folding booms or manually erected lattice booms simplify the procedure for covering a large area and for placing concrete into inaccessible areas.

The capacity of small-line pumps is infinitely variable up to about 76·5 m³ (100 yd³) per hour. This rating, however, depends entirely upon the ability of the ready mixed concrete supplier or batching plant to supply the necessary volume and on the efficiency of the contractor's placing gang. Distances of 274 m (900 ft) horizontally, or 76 m (250 ft) vertically, can be achieved with ease.

Successful operation of small-line pumping depends on the following factors:

1. Provision of a pump of required output, capable of applying pressure to, and displacing, concrete evenly and smoothly along the pipeline.
2. Erection of pipelines and booms to provide minimum frictional resistance within the capability of the pump and of the concrete.
3. Provision of 'pumpable' concrete and the evidence of marginal concrete causing excessive wear and increasing the possibility of breakdown.
4. Correct planning and liaison between the pumping specialist, the ready-mixed concrete supplier and the contractor.
5. Efficient pump operation and adequate maintenance.
6. Regular supply of concrete geared to match the capability of the placing gang. On large pours achieving a continuous truck discharge by having every truck discharging before the previous truck has completed its discharge.

The pumpability of concrete is of paramount importance in determining the success of a pour; the better the concrete, the easier the pour and the smaller the wear on the equipment. A concrete pump is only as good as the concrete going into it. The concrete mix is designed normally and then modified to give pumpable qualities. Concrete for pumping must be of the right consistency. The pump, in fact, provides its own quality control, rejecting mixtures that are too harsh, too wet, too dry, or badly graded, and accepting only concrete that has durability, workability, high density, low shrinkage, strength, cohesiveness and good finishing properties.

In the early days of pumping in the UK, the supply of 'pumpable' concrete was very much a 'hit or miss' affair. In these days, however, the vast majority of ready mixed concrete suppliers have standard pump mixes for all required strengths of concrete. If a contractor has any problems he should immediately contact the concrete pumping specialist who will in turn collaborate with the ready mix supplier.

It must be emphasised that pumping calls for competent mix design, and for a refusal to try to by-pass the known criteria. Whereas all good concrete is not necessarily pumpable, it is true to say that pumpable concrete must be good concrete. The types of cement suitable for pumping are Portland blast furnace cement, low-heat Portland cement, ordinary Portland cement, and sulphate-resisting cement. Aggregates which are suitable for dense concrete, such as sand, gravel and crushed rock, should be used. The aggregates differ in their geometric shape and individual hardness but their hardness has no effect on the pumpability. The future of concrete pumping in the UK is now established and during the next few years it will surely be one of the major growth industries within the construction industry. The time will almost certainly come when customers order pumping in the same way as they order ready mixed concrete. The pumps will be radio controlled and will probably be directed to four or five different sites in one day, pumping 11·5 m³ (15 yd³) on one site, 9·5 m³ (12 yd³) on the next, and so on, at very reasonable rates, thus making pumping economical for the small building contractor.

Pumping Costs

We have established that pumping concrete is an up and coming thing in Britain, and probably in the rest of continental Europe too, and that it is widely applicable to sites of all sizes. Pumping concrete will show savings on virtually any contract, although it is initially more expensive as an operation *per se*. However, when all the other factors are taken into consideration, factors such as labour saving (biggest item on any contract), freeing of other plant for other work, speed of placing, etc., it soon becomes apparent that this is a money saver. So little preparation is required on site: the pump can be ready in five minutes and can place up to 55·08 m³ (72 yd³) per hour. It really does not matter how much concrete is involved but a good average daily pour of 66·8–84·15 m³ (90–110 yd³) is most economical and, at current rates in Britain, would cost £70–£80 per day to hire. Placing by traditional means with crane and skip would probably be restricted to about 7·5–9·5 m³ (10–12 yd³) per hour but by pump this would be trebled or even quadrupled. When contractors used the method for the A2 bridge work it cost about £300–£400 per hour but time saved was estimated at about two-thirds.

Operating with two men on eight hours pumping, a Mark-Thomsen 740C would cost, on a 100 m³ (130 yd³) pour, £85, say 85p per metre, and that would involve a minimum charge of £75. Prices, of course, vary with site conditions and quantity of pour, but comparison can be made with the current purchase price of the MT 740C which is £17 000. Of that figure about £1500 should be allocated for spares and repairs during its life which will be three to five years. A plant-hire company would depreciate this machine over three years in all probability, while an owner-contractor might write it off over five years.

In some cases special rates are applied for hire throughout the

Figure 5.2. *Jetting pump for miniwell installation (courtesy Hüdig KG)*

Figure 5.3. *Main suction pump for dewatering installation*

entire concreting programme on a project. These usually range from £250–£330 per week, with no limit imposed on the amount of concrete pumped. On a large concreting job over a moderately lengthy period this can be a very favourable system to adopt, although the chances are that such circumstances run extremely close to a situation where the contractor would be better advised to purchase his own machine.

Dewatering Sites

The control of the land water table in many countries presents many problems. Astronomical sums of money are spent in the conservation of water but if nature produces abnormally wet weather periods, our waterways cannot handle the excess of water, and flooding occurs.

In low-lying areas, particularly, it causes disruption of traffic and delay in many industries, especially the construction industry. This means that some folk are being caused big financial headaches.

Methods of Control

To combat the water problem on construction sites there are a number of methods (Figures 5.2 to 5.4) which can be used and these are described as follows:

1(a).   The caisson installation and blowing the water out by use of compressed air.
1(b).   Pumping by submersible pumps.
2.   Using a series of centrifugal pumps and discharging the water on to lower levels or into convenient rivers or sewers.
3.   Installing a series of miniwells or dewatering system. This is probably the most effective way of handling water from a depth of around 8–10 m, depending on the ground strata, and is the method most suitable for gravel and sand-bearing grounds; denser strata can be dealt with, provided that the riser pipes can be inserted into the ground.

The first two methods of control are very well known to most contracting personnel and need not be enlarged upon.

The third method is not so well known, although there are three suppliers of this type of equipment in the UK. The miniwell system is also known as the shallow-well method. Their effective depth is 8–10 m, the latter figure being the absolute maximum; if the ground is waterlogged below that depth and it is necessary to work at lower levels then it is possible to handle the water in steps which means a second and possibly a third well installation.

The suction capacity of the pumps used in this method is limited to a maximum depth of 9 m. Down to a depth of 5 m the gravity action of the water is sufficient for the suction pump to cope; below that depth a vacuum pump has to be installed in the system.

Miniwells are particularly suitable for dewatering fine-sand soils with flux properties and a permeability range from $K = 10^{-3}$ to $K = 10^{-5}$ m^3/sec.

Figure 5.4. *Wellpoints in place stretching diagonally across the picture taken on a continental site*

Although miniwells are also used in coarse sand, fine gravel and for gravity dewatering they are still referred to as vacuum installations. Their potential has been increased by giving them greater intake scope, and by improving the equipment (particularly the vacuum pump) it has become possible to achieve a negative pressure of 9·6 m. These improvements, together with better filter materials,

Table 5.1. TABLE FOR ESTIMATION OF WATER QUANTITY

Soils	Clay	Silt			Sand			Gravel			Boulders
		Fine	Medium	Coarse	Fine	Medium	Coarse	Fine	Medium	Coarse	
Size, mm	less than 0·002	0·002 0·006	0·006 0·02	0·02 0·06	0·06 0·2	0·2 0·6	0·6 2·00	2 6	6 20	20 60	over 60
Permeability, K = cm/sec	10^{-9} to 10^{-6}	10^{-5}	10^{-4}	10^{-3}	10^{-2}	10^{-1}	1	>1			
1	0·01	0·30	0·40	0·70	1·40	2·70	5·00				
2		0·30	0·45	1·00	1·70	3·30	5·80				
3		0·40	0·50	1·20	2·10	4·10	6·70				
4		0·40	0·55	1·40	2·60	5·00	7·80				
5		0·40	0·60	1·60	3·20	6·10	8·10				
6		0·40	0·60	1·75	3·90	7·30	9·70				
7		0·40	0·60	1·90	4·70	8·70	10·70				
8		0·40	0·60	2·00	5·60	10·40	14·30				
9	0·20	0·40	0·60	2·10	6·60	12·50	17·70				

Water amount per running metre of lowering depth in canal building depth

Note 1 (a)   Note 2 (a)   Note 3 (a)   Notes 3 (b), 4 (a), 4 (b)   Note 2 (b)   Note 1 (b)   Note 1 (c)

Notes: 1 (a) Open water control, if not tidal water.
(b) Open water control, if water table does not need to be lowered more than 0·30 m.
(c) Open water control, with suitable trench shoring.
2 (a) Miniwell-vacuum method, installation on two sides, distance 0·6–1 m.
(b) Miniwell-gravity method, up to a water amount of 6 m³/h per running metre lowering distance. 1- or 2-sided installations according to water quantity and lowering depth.
3 (a) Miniwell-combination well method, in varying strata, especially when there is more than one water table.
(b) Miniwell-combination well method, for water amounts of up to 15 m³/h per metre of lowering distance.
4 (a) Shallow well installation, for lowering the water table up to about 5 m in one operation.
(b) Deep well installation, equipped with U-pumps for depths greater than 5 m in one operation.

allow stabilisation and dewatering of soils with K values of 10^{-6} to 10^{-8}. Refer to Table 5.1 for calculations and quantities.

Figure 5.5 illustrates vacuum dewatering.

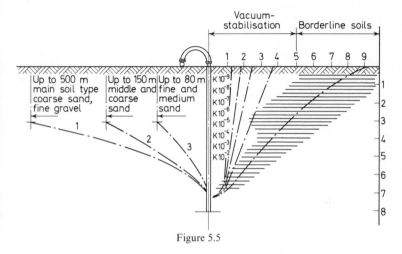

Figure 5.5

We speak of vacuum dewatering when there is adhesion in the soil and this means that a state of equilibrium exists between the capacity of each grain to hold water and the influence of gravity; this prevents water from flowing freely as the water has to carry sand grains with it. This phenomenon occurs in soils with K values ranging between 10^{-3} and 10^{-8}. If such soils are to be dewatered the essential function of the miniwell system is to produce a negative pressure in the soil. In this way, additional hydraulic pressure can attract the water attaching to the grains of sand and direct it towards the vacuum well. The soil is pressed against the well by an even atmospheric pressure and made workable. A further difference exists between vacuum and gravity dewatering and miniwell systems in construction and in the attainable lowering depth, allowing for water yield (see Tables 5.2 to 5.4).

If a miniwell system is employed in soils with $K = 10^{-3}$ then we are dealing with gravity dewatering. Miniwells can be used for gravity dewatering with water amounts of up to 10 m³/h running metre of lowering depth. The advantage of the miniwell over the shallow-well system lies in the fact that a negative pressure can be maintained in the former, thus allowing a faster rate of inflow. This has the effect of reducing the steepness of the slope of the excavation; and because miniwells are placed closer together the lowering parabola of the crater can be kept shallower.

Table 5.2

Type of Soil	Clay	Silt Fine	Medium	Coarse
Grain size up to mm	<0·002	0·002 0·006	0·006 0·02	0·002 0·06
$K=$ cm/sec	10^{-9} to 10^{-6}	10^{-5}	10^{-4}	10^{-3}
Well distance	0·60 m	0·60 m	1 m	1 m
Installation in trenches	Both sided	Both sided	Both sided	Both sided
Excavations of up to 3 m depth with a channel width of 1–2 m	—	—	—	One sided
Maximum lowering pump base (see Figure 5.6)	7·3 m	7·3 m	7·1 m	6–7 m

Table 5.3

M³/h per running metre lowering depth	1	1·5	2	2·5	3	4	5	6	7	8	9
Obtainable lowering depth, in metres	7	6·7	6·6	6·3	5·9	5·9	5·5	4·5			
Considered diameter of header manifold for 25 m in one flow direction	108	108	133	133	133	159	159	159			
Filter distance, in metres	2·5	1·8	1·3	1	1	1	0·8	0·8			
Installation one side only	X	X	X	X	X	X	X	X			

Table 5.4

M³/h per running metre lowering depth	1·5	2	2·5	3	4	5	6	7	8	9
Obtainable lowering depth, in metres	7	7	6·9	6·7	6·6	6·3	5·9	5·4	5·3	5·2
Header manifold diameter to be considered for a part distance of 25 m in one flow direction	108	108	108	108	133	133	133	133	159	159
Filter distance, in metres	3	2·5	2	1·8	1·3	1	1	1	1	0·8
Installation on two sides	X	X	X	X	X	X	X	X	X	X

Consequently, miniwells facilitate the lowering of the water table by depths exceeding those by shallow wells by up to 2 m (Figures 5.6). The filter area lies at a higher level in the miniwell than it does in the shallow-well system.

To achieve an equal lowering depth, the water quantities to be dealt with are smaller in miniwell installations, thus making running costs less for equal results (see Table 5.2).

There are certain conditions to be met when considering the installation of a miniwell. In brief, they are: (a) a pumping sample

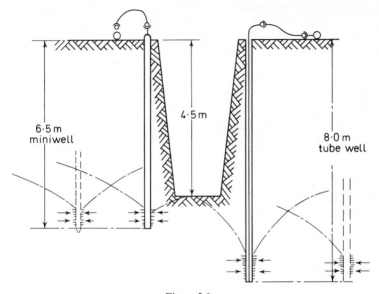

Figure 5.6

analysis should be made; (b) a sedimentation test should be made; (c) Table 5.1 assists in determining K value and water quantity.

A sedimentation test in which 60% of the particles are smaller than 0·2 mm suggests the use of shock-resistant plastic filter with aperture size 0·2 mm and, in addition, shrouding with filter sand containing a mixture of grains of size 1–3 mm. The thickness of the shroud should be 200 mm on all sides.

Performance of the miniwell can be increased if, during the jetting process, attention is given to the natural deposition of filter sand. Its effectiveness must be maintained by starting to operate the system in the correct manner.

Vacuum pumps and efficiently sealed pipe systems are prerequisites for the achievement of maximum lowering depth, as shown in Table 5.2. The dimensions of the header manifold pipe must not be of a lower order, otherwise loss through friction could become too great. To accomplish a lowering of the water table to a depth of 7·3 m it is necessary to have a negative pressure of 8·8 m at the end of the header manifold, at which point a vacuum gauge must be used.

In the vacuum method the ultimate lowering depth depends on particle size and K value. In gravity methods it depends on quantity of water and on pressure losses due to friction in the suction line as well as in the header pipe manifold.

The given maximum lowering depth can only be obtained if vacuum pumps are used as well as completely sealed pipelines and if the diameter of the header manifold is appropriate to the water yield.

Maximum lowering depth is always taken to be the distance from the bottom of the excavation to the inlet cock of the vacuum pump (see Figure 5.7).

The level of the groundwater is of no consequence in this context. If the lowered water table lies at levels of 1 m, 2 m, or 3 m below

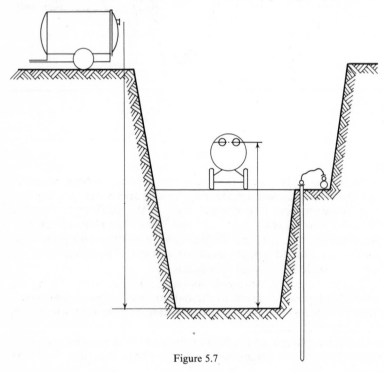

Figure 5.7

ground the performance of the installation can be improved by placing the pump lower on a shelf.

Table 5.4 gives filter distances. These are based on the assumption that the intake of each miniwell in a gravity system consists of 3 m³/h. In determining the covering suitable for the filters it is necessary to take into consideration the height of the water table which must be lowered (see Table 5.5). 'Covering' means the distance between top of filter and floor of excavation.

Table 5.5

Water Yield		10^{-9} to 10^{-4}	10^{-3}	2 m³/h	2–4 m³/h	4 m³/h
Height of	1 m	1·2 m	1·5 m	1·5 m	1·4 m	1·2 m
water table to be	1–2 m	1·0 m	1·2 m	1·2 m	1·2 m	1·0 m
lowered	2–3 m	0·8 m	1·0 m	1·0 m	1·0 m	0·8 m
	>3 m	0·6 m	0·6 m	1·0 m	0·8 m	0·7 m

The tables supply some information for the employment of mini-wells, and indicate how systems should be installed in different soil conditions and what maximum lowering distances can be reached. However, the following is a rule-of-thumb formula for the relationship between filter distance and covering in the installation of miniwells: filter covering=1 m when filter distance is between 1 and 2 m and can be applied when maximum performance is not essential. Nevertheless, the prescribed filter distance should be adhered to for reasons of margins of error and economy.

As stated before, a vacuum gauge must be incorporated at the end of the header manifold and, during the middle phase of dewatering, this must register a negative pressure of 1 m greater than the geodetic suction lifting height, measured from the tip of the filter to the header manifold pipe.

Installation

Vacuum method—two sided
Gravity method—one sided

When operating with miniwells in conditions of coarse sand and of gravel, and a lowering depth of 3–4 m is exceeded, it will be necessary, with the aid of a sedimentation test, to work out the probable water amount and to install the plant absolutely correctly according to the tables given.

CHAPTER SIX

Plant Selection and Costing

Heavy construction plant has become a considerable drain on a company's resources, and with high interest rates on borrowed money and other restrictions on capital it is essential to attend to the following:

1. Tender for and obtain contracts that will ensure the majority of the plant fleet being reasonably utilised.
2. Make a careful study of manufacturers' products to choose machines with economical features in operation and maintenance.
3. Have a 100% maintenance organisation.

Government investment allowance, tax relief and inland revenue tax payable on plant investments require balancing, in conjunction with the plant fleet and labour force employed.

Due to some unfortunate period during the life of a contract, perhaps bad weather or unforeseen site-ground conditions which can add to operation costs or labour troubles, contributing to prolonging the time-cycle, it may be necessary for a contractor to purchase additional machines. This may save the contractor from penalty payments but, due to increased investment and interest charges in relation to cash flow, may reduce his net profit for a particular contract. Naturally, at the estimating stage, it is as well to have clauses in the tender documents which give some protection in instances of this nature. Investment in new plant should have a percentage ratio to the fixed assets of a company, and the general ratio in the UK of sizeable companies is about $1\frac{1}{2}$–3% building content and 15–30% plant. It will also have to bear some relationship to the costs and revenue from current contracts.

Finance that has to be obtained to augment income must come from the most economical market. Additional sources of income, such as investments, play some part in the overall picture, but cash flow is influenced in many ways, some of which can be listed under the following headings: (*a*) under-certification of completed work; (*b*) dilatory payments of certificates; (*c*) increased plant costs due to site conditions; (*d*) stoppages to work flow due to innumerable

Figure 6.1. *Light derrick crane assisting erection of larger derrick crane on high building contract (courtesy John Laing and Son Ltd.)*

causes; (*e*) indifferent planning at the commencement of the contract, weather hold-ups, machine breakdowns. These are a few of the factors which curtail the flow of money and seriously restrict company finances.

Plant usage and life are two important features in the economics of a company. Profitability is influenced by a machine's working cycle and to illustrate this situation a few examples of various types of machine and reasons for monetary results being affected are given:

1. Machines such as Scotch Derrick Cranes, which do not have fast-moving units and are constructed of structural steel, usually have a much longer working life-cycle than heavy earthmoving machinery (Figure 6.1). Provided normal maintenance is carried out, there should be no need for expensive repairs or overhauls. Taking heavy earthmoving machinery as another example, this requires maintenance on a much more expensive scale, and, in addition, after about 3000 h operation will require a complete overhaul, which usually is a high cost operation. The latter costs have been reduced somewhat by the introduction of higher grade steel in the components, life-time bearings and better designed units, allowing the user to renew a complete unit without having the extra cost of a stripping down before being able to carry out repairs. There are other contributory factors to cost saving such as:

2. A well-planned preventive maintenance scheme, influenced by periodic inspections by competent construction plant engineers.

3. Site personnel responsible for conditions should be schooled in taking an interest in machine performances and co-operating with the mechanical engineering staff in maintaining good ground surfaces for machines which have to operate in fast-cycle sequences in order to keep down operating costs. This also ensures a minimum of downtime due to breakages and damage to running gear, tyre wear, etc.

4. A company should have skilled operators and if they do not have the facilities for training their own they should use the Government training schools, privately run facilities, or enlist the services of the manufacturer. A competent operator can save a company much money, both by his skill in operating his machine, and by taking an interest in seeing that normal routine maintenance is carried out regularly and thoroughly.

The yearly working cycle of machines differs considerably due to climatic conditions. Some plant can operate in adverse weather and site situations, but they are in a minority. Also, the geographical situation of sites has an effect on the annual working periods of a contract. Marine work is governed by the seasons. Usually sites have to curtail their operations during the winter months and a good average working year is between 35 and 40 weeks. During the better weather periods, the financial return can be influenced by double shifting, especially where bulk excavation is involved.

The majority of the leading contractors, and particularly the hiring companies in the UK, adopt a replacement schedule of three, five or ten years, depending on size and type of machine. A more detailed exposition of the economics involved is given at the end of this chapter.

Plant Replacement

Replacement of plant is a most controversial subject and a number of factors must be taken into account. These include the following: (a) depreciation; (b) cost of replacement, bearing in mind increased purchase prices; (c) cost of interest charges on money; (d) cost of maintenance; (e) cost of downtime, either caused through weather/site conditions or machine breakdown.

There is a period when costs, fixed and operating, begin to balance amortisation values and, from an economic point of view, this would appear to be the time to consider selling a machine. Moreover, manufacturers may have produced a more up-to-date machine in the interim, making the one under consideration obsolete.

Plant Provision

Plant is provided from a variety of sources and these can include: (a) from a company's own plant holdings; (b) hired in from specialist or general plant-hiring companies; (c) purchased on extended terms; (d) purchased outright with some help from Government investment grants where applicable; (e) leased on guaranteed buy-back arrangements. The latter method has the advantage of a fixed depreciation cost, but a disadvantage in that higher maintenance costs may be incurred in order to hand back a machine in a condition required to qualify for the agreed buy-back price. It also restricts having a change of supplier if conditions become strained.

Reference has been made to 'plant utilisation' earlier in the book and the importance of this cannot be stressed too strongly. Personnel responsible for planting a contract must keep it well in mind when deciding what to purchase, what to hire in and what to obtain on lease. If it can be seen that a machine has a general-purpose utility, then it is more economical to purchase and, quite probably, on a buy-back arrangement. Where machines have a limited use, then the hiring in method is certainly the sensible approach. Another side of the problem is duration of the work in hand; this will have some bearing on how to deal with the situation.

Plant Department Budgeting

In Chapter 7 we have shown how to prepare a budgeting control system. In this chapter we will refer only to the points which go to make up a workable budget system. A plant department's financial activity is related to an annual budget and primary factors affecting it include:

1. Long-range forecasts are linked with short-term policies for existing contracts.
2. Plant holdings have to be replaced based on utilisation periods and residual values.
3. High-percentage utilisation affects a company's ability when tendering for new contracts.
4. Capital availability controls the purchasing power of a plant department.
5. An efficient costing system based on a plant department's machine records.
6. A plant department should be kept fully in the overall picture to enable it to produce its yearly budget and to be advised of the forward thinking of the management.
7. Budgets are greatly influenced by manufacturers' activities and a close liaison should be kept by plant department personnel with manufacturer's programmes. This will enable them to build into budget calculations the probable increase in machine purchasing costs.

Plant Purchasing

Machine replacement is closely related to forward thinking by company management. This involves the plant department in many considerations which may be categorised under:

1. Type and quantity of work envisaged over a given period.
2. The company policy on plant replacement, together with manufacturer's plans for production of new or modified machine models.

3. Consideration to be given to existing plant holdings when considering new purchases.
4. In the UK Government investment allowance, tax allowances, bank interest rates, all play an important part when new plant is being considered.
5. Close checks of hired plant rates should be made to compare the possibility of using hired plant as opposed to the purchasing of plant.
6. Machine characteristics examined to enable a careful appraisement to be made regarding outputs and, in turn, financial reward as opposed to capital outlay.

Plant Hire

In the UK today there is a growing tendency for contracting companies to sub-contract the bulk earthmoving work to specialist firms who have, over the years, built up a reputation for this type of work and can give a knowledgeable estimate of cost per unit cubic metre or tonnage. In addition, the contractors have also formed departments in their own organisations to deal with specialist work, such as soil mechanics, tunnelling, mass concreting, etc. In doing this, they have also turned to contract hire, particularly for the expensive items of plant, even though knowing full well it is not a cheap form of operation, but at least they have the knowledge of firm and stable costs per unit measurement guaranteed.

Contractors have also formed their own hire departments and the latter have to compete with the national hiring companies, so that the contractor is well catered for, whichever way he wishes to plant a site. In addition to these two suppliers of plant, specialised or conventional, there are some manufacturers who, to popularise their products, operate in the plant-hire markets. They tend to keep to the more expensive heavy plant knowing that smaller conventional plant is cut to ribbons financially.

Plant Costing

This comes under a number of headings:

1. Fixed costs—these are incurred whether the machine is working or standing.
   (a) Net capital cost after deduction of grants, tax allowances and residual values.

(*b*) Bank interest charges, administration expenses, insurances, licences, etc.

2. Operating costs—these are influenced by utilisation, weather and site conditions, operator efficiency and include:

(*a*) Fuel, oil and consumable stores.

(*b*) Repairs—spares, labour and supervision.

(*c*) Transportation costs.

(*d*) Erection and dismantling costs where applicable.

(*e*) Any other expenses which are necessary for the efficient operation of machines.

3. Workshop and maintenance costs.

(*a*) Workshop installations, e.g. cleaning facilities, which can be expensive if thoroughly done. Stripping down bays, structural steel bay, including welding shop, assembly bays. Testing facilities. Paint shop. Stores for spare parts; store space for structural steel. The larger companies segregate engine repair facilities from the machine repair shop. An inspection department is probably added to the above, particularly when full reconditioning of plant is carried out. Training of personnel comes under this cost heading. The larger companies have training schemes for their fitters and other artisans. The construction industry in the UK has followed other industries and has training facilities for craftsmen and this includes all trades and drivers of machines. It is in its infancy so far, but is being built up into an efficient service to the industry. Companies are levied per head of employees and can reclaim some of the expense when their staff are using the training scheme.

Estimating Costs of Ownership and Operating

Most manufacturers of equipment have, at some time or another, formulated cost-estimating procedures for the benefit of users of their equipment. Their experience is wide and their resources are often impressive so users, whether owners or hirers, seldom have the opportunity to better their advice. In particular the American manufacturers and their subsidiary companies deserve recognition for the publications they make available. They seem to be more ready than those of some other countries to accept the obvious fact that the better the general standard of education of the plant user, the better off is their industry as a whole and, therefore, the greater their opportunity to benefit individually. Why some plant producers are so reluctant to accept this is hard to understand, but there it is, a fact of civil engineering life—secretive they are and thus they seem prepared to remain, firm in the belief that the less they tell, the more they keep from their competitors.

So it is with acknowledgement to the companies who have been less reticent and who have not only subsidised the preliminary work of calculation but who have permitted its reproduction outside of their own sales forces, that we offer some of the following guides to ownership and operating cost estimating. It should be noted that although some of the following examples refer specifically to certain types of equipment they are, nevertheless, a sound foundation for indicating how users can set out their own methods and apply them to other items of plant used on civil engineering and building sites.

In their advice to users to find ownership costs, Terex GM point out that the purpose of the following cost-estimating system is to establish a relative comparison between two or more earthmoving vehicles. This system does not determine the total cost for any earthmoving operation. It does not include the cost of loading (except for pushloading scrapers with crawler tractors), supervision, general overhead, spreading, compaction, haul road construction and its maintenance, etc. Also, any estimates made according to the methods presented here are not be construed as specific guarantees of production rates or cost. This system of estimating hourly ownership and operating costs should be used only as a guide. Actual items of cost should be used whenever they are available to the estimator.

The cost of moving a quantity of material is determined by dividing the hourly cost of ownership and operation (0 & 0) by the hourly production:

$$\text{Cost per unit of material} = \frac{\text{Hourly cost of ownership and operation}}{\text{Hourly production}}$$

The first half of an 0 & 0 estimate is the ownership cost. It is the sum of the hourly charges for depreciation, interest, taxes, insurance and storage. The hourly depreciation charge is the delivered price of the unit (less the value of the tyres if a rubber-tyred unit—tyre costs are shown in costs of operation), divided by the depreciation period in hours. A straight-line method with no salvage or resale value is usually used and is considered good practice.

Five items are necessary to make the depreciation calculation. They are: purchase price, extras, freight, tyre costs and the depreciation period.

Purchase price may be the dealer's quote or taken directly from the price list, while *extras* include options and attachments necessary for the machine to perform well and necessary for the comfort of the operator. Care should be taken to see that the machine is properly equipped and that the costs for each item are included. Set-up charges should be included in this section.

Freight costs can be estimated most accurately by the person responsible for paying them. The costs for loading, blocking, unloading, special permits, or driver and vehicle expenses in the case of a customer drive-away, should be included.

Tyre costs should be obtained from the local tyre distributor or the average contractor replacement price shown in the equipment handbook can be used for estimating purposes.

The *depreciation period* is difficult to determine since useful life can exceed the depreciation period by a considerable amount if a good preventive maintenance programme is employed. Most customers will have a period they want to use based on their own experience. The figures in Table 6.1 may be used in lieu of contractor preference. These figures are not meant to designate any legal depreciation periods for tax purposes.

Table 6.1

Total depreciation period (hours)	Number of operating hours per year	Number of years write-off	Type of equipment
10 000	2 000	5	Contracting service: rear dump, bottom dump, scraper, crawler, tractor, loader
15 000	3 000	5	Industrial service: rear dump, bottom dump

In determining the cost of interest on the equipment investment, taxes on the assessed valuation of the equipment, cost of insurance premiums for general liability, fire, theft, etc., and cost of storage of the equipment, the following formula is used:

$$\text{Hourly cost of interest, taxes, insurance, storage} = \frac{\text{Prevailing rate (\%)} \times \text{Av. yearly investment}}{\text{Hours operated per year}}$$

There are numerous values for *prevailing rate* in use throughout the construction industry. Most authorities agree the current prevailing rate is 13%, made up of 9% for interest, 2% for taxes, and 2% for insurance and storage.

To determine *average yearly investment,* simply multiply the

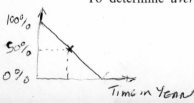

delivered price by 50% The following examples show why the average yearly investment is 50% of the initial investment (delivered price) regardless of the number of years to complete write-off.

5 YEARS TO COMPLETE WRITE-OFF   2 YEARS TO COMPLETE WRITE-OFF

Year	Value at Middle of Year	Year	Value at Middle of Year
1	90% of original investment	1	75% of original investment $\left(\frac{100+50}{2}\right)$
2	70%	2	25%
3	50%		100% ÷ 2 years = 50% of
4	30%		initial investment
5	10%		

250% ÷ 5 years = 50% of
          initial investment

$$\text{Interest, taxes, insurance, storage} = \frac{13\% \times 50\% \times \text{delivered price}}{\text{Hours operated per year}}$$

For example, to find the hourly ownership cost for an American vehicle with a delivered price of $80 000, depreciated over a five-year period, working 2000 h per year (tyre replacement costs are $12 000):— see prev page.

$$\text{Depreciation} = \frac{\$80\,000 - \$12\,000}{10\,000\,\text{h}} = \frac{\$68\,000}{10\,000\,\text{h}} = \$6.80/\text{h}$$

$$\text{Interest, taxes insurance, storage} = \frac{50\% \times \$80\,000 \times 13\%}{2000\,\text{h}} = \$2.60/\text{h}$$

The total ownership cost for such a machine will then be: $6.80 + $2.60 = $9.40/h.

Tyre Life

Table 6.2 represents the ranges of tyre life on favourable, average or unfavourable jobs. If job conditions are well known, the tyre life factor method previously discussed should be used. In the absence of such knowledge, Table 6.2 will provide an estimate.

Table 6.2. RANGES OF TYRE LIFE

Vehicle	Working conditions, in hours		
	Favourable	Average	Unfavourable*
Scrapers, twin	4 000	3 000	2 500
Scrapers, single			
tractor	4 000	3 000	2 500
scraper	5 500	3 500	2 500
Loaders	4 000	3 500 – 3 000	2 500 – 1 000
Rear dumps	4 000	3 500 – 3 000	2 500 – 2 000
Bottom dumps	8 000	5 000	3 500

*Poor haul road maintenance can result in even lower tyre-life figures.

Recapping–Retreading Costs

According to industry averages, 75 % of all tyres can be recapped if this is done before the tread is worn down into the casing. Costs for this average about 50 % of the original value of the tyre. Recap life is computed, again as an average, between 75 % and 85 % of the original tread life. Rarely will tubeless tyres require the addition of tubes and a rim modification when they are recapped.

Based on this, the average cost for tyre replacement including re-capping, say the Americans, may be found by multiplying the original tyre replacement hourly cost by a factor of 0·8. Thus, in the Terex calculations, a tyre replacement cost for the original set of tyres of $3.00/h would be reduced to an average tyre replacement cost of $2.40 ($3.00 × 0·8) for the original set plus recaps.

When exact recapping cost and life is known or can be accurately projected, the following formula can be applied:

$$\frac{\text{Replacement cost} + \text{Recap cost*}}{\text{Original life} + \text{Recap life}} = \text{Hourly tyre cost}$$

Tyre Repair Cost

In estimating total tyre cost, it is customary to apply a certain margin of safety in the form of tyre repair cost:

Hourly tyre repair cost = Tyre repair factor × Hourly tyre replacement cost

General working conditions	Tyre repair factor (with or without recapping), %
Favourable	12
Average	15
Unfavourable	17

General Repairs

This item includes parts and labour cost involved in normal maintenance and periodic overhaul of the vehicle. General repairs should be based on actual experience. However, an hourly charge can be established for estimating purposes by using the hourly depreciation charge of the unit as being indicative of the repair costs. Wide ex-

*This cost reflects the addition of a tube and modification of the rim if necessary.

perience of earthmoving operations over a great number of years shows that the average hourly repair cost can be determined very simply as a percentage of 10 000h depreciation charge. Although the unit depreciation is figured on the basis of some other time period, repair costs should be estimated as a percentage of 10 000h depreciation cost. The final factor in the expression below accounts for this.

$$\begin{matrix} \text{Hourly} \\ \text{cost of} \\ \text{general} \\ \text{repairs} \end{matrix} = \begin{matrix} \text{Repair} \\ \text{factor } (\%) \end{matrix} \times \begin{matrix} \text{Hourly} \\ \text{depreciation} \\ \text{cost} \end{matrix} = \frac{\text{Depreciation period (in hours)}}{10\,000 \text{ h}}$$

Selection of the percentage to be applied is a matter of judgement. The combined effect of such operating conditions as type of preventive maintenance, operator technique, payloads, applications, haul road conditions, etc., should be considered to determine whether favourable, average or unfavourable condition percentages should be used. Experience has shown that crawler tractor repair costs vary greatly across a wide range of applications. This experience is reflected in Table 6.3. Note also that crawler hourly depreciation costs are based on list prices. There are no tyres to delete.

Table 6.3. REPAIR FACTORS

Based on a depreciation period of 10 000 h	Favourable conditions %	Average conditions %	Unfavourable conditions %
Scrapers, all types	42	50	62
Front-end loaders, rubber-tyred	45	55	70
Rear dumps	37	45	60
Bottom dumps	30	35	45
Crawler tractors (by application)			
industrial	10	25	75
general contracting	40	60	80
quarrying	50	85	115
mining	70	110	150
logging	55	135	215

Another American manufacturer, the International Harvester Company, offer the following methods for assessing depreciation costs on machines on which hourly rates may be calculated.

The hourly charge for machine depreciation is found by dividing the machine's delivered price by the anticipated hours of useful life. The delivered price of a machine is f.o.b. factory price plus freight charges. Tyre prices, however, should be deducted from the delivered price of wheeled machines since it is usual for tyres to be treated as operating cost items and having no bearing on machine depreciation.

Next, a method of depreciating the machine over its useful life must be considered to arrive at an hourly charge rate. To see how these differ, assume a piece of equipment with a delivered price (less tyres) of £15 000, a depreciation period of 5 years, and with no allowance for salvage. Any of the rates of depreciation given in Table 6.4 may be used; a depreciation guide for specific equipment is given in Table 6.5.

Table 6.4. METHODS OF MACHINE DEPRECIATION

Year	Straight-line method £	Declining balance method £	Sum-of-the-years digit method £
1	3 000	6 000	5 000
2	3 000	3 600	4 000
3	3 000	2 160	3 000
4	3 000	1 296	2 000
5	3 000	778	1 000
Total	£15 000	£13 834	£15 000

The 'sum-of-the-years digit method' allows the owner to depreciate his equipment more rapidly during the early years of the machine's life than is possible under the 'straight-line method'. For example, if the machine is to be depreciated over 5 years, the first step is to add up the digits $(1+2+3+4+5)=15$. In the first year, the machine has, naturally, 5 years in which to be depreciated; therefore, the allowable depreciation for the first year will be $\frac{5}{15}$ of the delivered price. Similarly, at the start of the second year, the machine has 4 years remaining in which to be depreciated; therefore the allowable depreciation is equal to $\frac{4}{15}$ of the delivered price; at the start of the third year $\frac{3}{15}$, etc. As can be seen in the above example,

Table 6.5 DEPRECIATION GUIDE

I-H machine	Operating Conditions					
	Poor		Average		Excellent	
	years	hours	years	hours	years	hours
Crawler tractors	4	8 000	5	10 000	6	12 000
Crawler loaders	4	8 000	5	10 000	6	12 000
Crawlers and sidebooms			6	12 000		
Crawler-drawn scrapers	5	10 000	6	12 000	7·5	15 000
Cable and hydraulic control units			5	10 000		
Blades	4	8 000	5	10 000		
Pay scrapers	4	8 000	5	10 000	6	12 000
Pay haulers	4	8 000	5	10 000	7·5	15 000
Pay loaders	4	8 000	5	10 000	6	18 000
Pay dozers	4	8 000	5	10 000	6	12 000

the sum-of-the-years digit method allows the owner to depreciate £9000 in the first two years as opposed to £6000 under the straight-line method. It should also be noted that the sum-of-the-years digit method enables the owner to completely depreciate the cost of the equipment.

The 'declining balance method' allows the owner to depreciate a much higher amount during the first few years of the machine's life expectancy and, naturally, a lesser amount during the latter years of the machine's life. Firstly, with this system, estimate the number of years of machine life and then establish the percentage applicable under the straight-line method. For example, by the straight-line method of depreciation a period of five years allows the owner to depreciate at the rate of 20% of the cost per year. The declining balance method allows him to depreciate at double the straight-line rate, *but only on the balance* of the cost remaining after subtracting any depreciation already taken. In Table 6.4, by the straight-line method, the owner can depreciate 20% of the £15 000 in the first year (£3000). For the declining balance method the owner doubles this 20% to 40% and, as a result, can depreciate £6000 in the first year (40% of £15 000). At the start of the second year the balance of the price remaining is £9000 (£15 000–£6000). He then takes 40% of the remaining £9000 and a depreciation of £3600. As is shown, at no time can one ever depreciate the entire cost of the machine. However, the method does allow the option of fast depreciation in the early years of life.

For the purpose of estimating, the straight-line method serves the estimator best because with it, depreciation is charged off at an even rate and unlike the declining balance method, leaves no un-claimed balance. At the same time it allows the estimator to establish an *average* hourly depreciation figure for any given period of machine life. However, the contractor may use variations of these methods, and when exact depreciation schedules are known they should be used for preference.

Under average operating conditions and an estimated useful life of 10 000h, average hourly depreciation cost is 10% of the total depreciation price.

Sheet Steel Piling

Another activity that is very commonly employed on both civil engineering construction and building sites is piling with sheet steel for the reinforcement of trenching and excavations. Because of the universal use of this system, irrespective of size, on small building

sites, local pipelaying contracts, or on large-scale projects such as
dams and bridges of the greatest magnitude, it was deemed worthy
of special consideration and space.

Much of the equipment involved in this operation in Britain is
hired but, of course, specialist contractors or the larger general

Figure 6.2. 43 m (141 ft) *high pile frame—one of the largest ever made (courtesy BSP
International Foundations Ltd.)*

contractors will most probably purchase their own. Figure 6.2
shows one of these exceptions. Made by BSP International Foundations Ltd., for Taylor Woodrow International, this is one of the
largest pile frames ever made, being 43 m (141 ft) in overall height.
On its 36 m (120 ft) span gantry its job was to drive 7000 prestressed
concrete piles, each measuring 33 m (110 ft) in length and 0·7 m
(27 in) diameter. It is generally considered, however, that 80% of
piling equipment used in Britain is hired and the strange fact that
emerged during the research for this book was that many contractors
owning their piling plant will often actually hire in more plant rather
than repair the material they have in stock. Vast quantities of piling
plant and material are lying around the country disused but in

repairable state while the owners are hiring other plant. The reason for this can be found in currently unrealistically low hire rates; it is more economic and less costly to hire locally. In some cases it seemed that the existing plant could be repaired at reasonable cost and it could only be deduced that management was at fault in not making use of what was available.

It is not usual for piling equipment to be hired out with an operator but drilling equipment does come with an operator because it is more sophisticated by nature. As a general rule, it is considered adequate for the hire company to make itself available in an advisory capacity.

Many types of sheeting are available for trench reinforcement, together with several techniques for driving, and to a large degree the selection of driving equipment also affects the sheeting capacity. It is important that the characteristics of the sheeting driver (impact rate and impact force) accord with the basic conditions, and that the transfer of energy from driver to the sheeting should take place under optimum conditions. The correct choice of guide for the driver is also important.

Wage costs are best calculated in terms of hourly pay, and are to be weighed against costs for more mechanised equipment.

In the following discussion, *wage costs* amount to 120p per man-hour. The *operational costs* include expenses for diesel and lubricating oil consumed. If the compressor is electrically powered, replace the diesel oil costs by those for electricity. With a compressor, operational costs amount to 40–70%.

As an example, the capacity in medium difficult soils of Atlas Copco compressed air powered sheeting drivers is given in Table 6.6. The tabulation has been based on empirical results from various sheeting operations.

Table 6.6

Driver type	Max. length trench sheeting m (ft)	Max. length light sections m (ft)	Max. weight heavy sections and special sheeting kg (lb)
TEP 40	3·0 (10)	—	60 (130)
TEP 100	4·5 (15)	4·5 (15)	150 (330)
TEP 400	5·5 (18)	6·5 (21)*	300 (660)
PH 180K	5·5 (18)	6·5 (21)*	600 (1 320)

*Also 'double sections'.

The available sheeting capacity can be calculated in sheeted area per time unit (m^2/h) as follows:

1. The net sheeting time (hours) per sheet pile during the work in question is made the object of a time study. To this is added the time required for transport, waiting, etc., giving the gross sheeting time (hours) per sheet pile.
2. The area of the sheet pile (m^2) is known and by multiplying the gross sheeting time per sheet pile by the area of the pile, the desired capacity figure is reached in terms of sheeted area *per time unit* (m^2/h).

Calculating Costs

To obtain an overall idea of costs involved in a sheeting operation, with a view to bringing them down to a minimum, it is obvious that mechanisation is the best way of reducing the labour item and to achieve this the most profitable combination has to be found. The costs for material and equipment are made up by the total of capital, operational and maintenance expenses. Capital costs are to be calculated with reference to the economical life of the sheeting and equipment. In sheeting work of medium difficulty, repair costs make up an average of 50–70% of capital costs.

Generally speaking, the economic yield can be calculated with the help of the measured cost per completed or sheeted unit area (cost/m^2). When the time required to complete the work is known (capacity), costs per time unit can be calculated:

$$\text{cost/h} = \text{m}^2/\text{h} \times \text{cost/m}^2$$

The lowest operational cost per square metre and highest capacity are reached with a double rig, but the highest costs result from the use of a free-riding driver. Rigging up the driver on a guide beam (on the excavating machine) is approximately 20% cheaper than using a free-riding driver. The qualitative result of operations is also better. It should be remembered that too small a compressor or hose size raises the costs per square metre, due to the appreciably lower capacity of the driver.

The figure for the monthly spare parts consumption is to be calculated in percentages of the present value of the machinery. Spare parts consumption can then most often be graphically approximated by a straight line. Under very difficult working conditions, extra costs of 50–100% should be taken into consideration.

For a hypothetical example, take a trench to be shored up with vertical sheeting. The soil is clayey sand with a relatively regular distribution of grain size and medium compactness. The water content is slight.

The trench is to be 1500 m long, 2 m wide, and 4 m deep and to be shored up 75 m at a time. The sheeting is then to be used $\frac{1500}{75}=20$ times. The time required for shoring is estimated at 50 days with one shift (8 h) operations.

The sheeting is to be driven vertically, before excavation:

Sheeting: Steel sheet piles HKD 400 length $=4.5$ m
width $=400$ mm
area $=1.8$ m^2
Walings: Steel walings IPB 140 length $=6.0$ m
width $=140$ mm
Quantity required: 26 pieces
Struts: Wooden struts with accessories (2.0 m long). Only one row of struts is required. 75 m of sheeting requires approx. 25–30 struts. The struts are to be secured with chains.

Thirty per cent of the sheeting is written off and 20 % of the remaining material. The higher depreciation for the sheeting is due to the fact that it is exposed to greater mechanical stresses and thus has a lower degree of utilisation.

No consideration is made of the scrap value of the sheeting. The write-off percentage is the basis for the factor by which the capital cost for sheeting material is to be multiplied, since the sheeting is to be used several times.

The factor is calculated as follows:

$$\frac{\text{Depreciation } (\%)}{100 \times \text{No. times material used}}$$

For the sheeting in this case: $\dfrac{30}{100 \times 20} = 0.015$

Remaining material: $\dfrac{20}{100 \times 20} = 0.010$

Capital costs for the sheeting material per m^2 (on the basis of price/weight) $=$ approx. £4 — 40/m^2, which, with consideration of the repeated use, gives a costs share of $0.015 \times$ £4 — 40 $= 6.60$p/m^2 sheeted surface.

The capital costs for the remaining sheeting material per m^2 sheeted surface $=$ approx. 112p.

Repeated use gives a cost of $0.010 \times$ £1—12 $= 1.12$p/m^2 sheeted surface.

Capital costs for sheeting material per m^2 sheeted surface $=$ approx. 8p/m^2.

These figures are to be considered normal values. In difficult soil conditions, the degree of utilisation for the sheeting drops, affecting the size of the depreciation factor.

Equipment (Compressed Air Driven)

The choice of equipment affects the economic result to a high degree. Given below, then, are a number of alternative combinations of equipment and the costs they entail. Affecting capital cost are the magnitude of the investment, length of the write-off period, rate of interest and degree of utilisation.

The yearly capital cost (annuity) is calculated by the following formula:

Annuity (progressive depreciation)=

$$\frac{[\text{Invested capital } (1+\text{Interest rate}) -\text{Scrap value}] \text{ Interest rate}}{\text{Write-off time}}$$

$$[(1+\text{Interest rate})-1] \text{ Utilisation factor} \times \text{No. of work-hours per normal year}$$

In this example, a normal case:

Write-off period:	3 years
Utilisation factor:	Compressor 0·7 (70%), remaining equipment 0·6 (60%)
Interest rate:	8%
Scrap value:	Nil
Normal year:	2000 work-hours

A sheeting driver, costing £800 used in the operation outlined above has a capital cost:

$$\text{Annuity}=\frac{[800(1+0·05)^5]\,0·05}{[(1+0·05)^5-1]\,0·60\times2000}=13·60\text{p/h}$$

Maintenance costs are calculated as a percentage increase of the annuity: 50–70% × capital costs.

In this example, 70%: $0·7\times1·70=25·60$p/h of capital costs. In this case, calculation is based on a figure of 60%.

Guide beams and rigs have no direct operational costs. The sheeting driver consumes lubricants, entailing an operational cost of 15–20% of the capital cost—here 20%.

In order to present a view of the total costs for different equipment, a capacity study (time study) and the following calculations of costs are given in Table 6.7 for seven equipment combinations. Because this information has its source in Sweden the cost examples in this section dealing with sheet-piling operations were originally quoted in Swedish crowns. The figures are related to 1970 values but neither the values themselves nor the form of currency in which they are expressed are relevant. Their significance lies in their proportion in the costing procedure. They were calculated and presented by Mr. Magnus Bergman and Atlas Copco MCT, by whose courtesy they are reproduced here, and for easier assimilation approximate conversions have been made into sterling equivalents.

In difficult operations, extra expenses from 50 to 100% may have to be added to the calculated values.

If net costs for the entire sheeting operation are desired, the ex-

Table 6.7

[handwritten: single – single acting compressed air m]
[handwritten: free riding – gravity]

Equipment							
Sheeting driver, weight in kg	75	150	400	400	400	2×400	2×400
Sheeting driver, guide mechanism	Single rig	Single rig	Free riding	Single rig	Guide beam on excavating machine	2×single rig	Double rig
Air consumption, m³/min	2·5	2·5	3·5	3·5	3·5	7·1	7·1
Work force, men per shift	2	2	3	2	2	3	2
Sheeting capacity							
Effective sheeting time, min	9·0	4·5	3·5	3·5	3·5	3·5	3·5
Extra time for transfers, min	2·0	2·0	5·0	2·0	3·0	2·5	2·0
	11·0	6·5	8·5	5·5	6·5	6·0	5·5
Number of sheet piles per hour	5·5	9	7	11	9	20	22
Capacity, m²/h	9·9	16·2	12·6	19·8	16·2	36·0	39·5
Cost Classification (£p/h)							
Sheeting driver							
Capital costs	10	12	26	26	26	52	52
Operational costs	2	2·4	6	6	6	12	12
Maintenance costs	7·2	8	18	18	18	36	36
Total, sheeting driver	19·2	22·4	50	50	50	100	100
Guide equipment							
Capital costs	38·8	38·8			52	36	£1.04	£1.04
Winch	8	8		8		2×8	2×10
Operational and maintenance costs	6	6		6		2×6	2×6
Excavating machine (rental)			£2.40		£3.20		
Total, guide equipment	52·8	52·8	£2.40	66	£3.56	£1.32	£1.36
Compressor							
Capital costs	28	30	42	42	42	72	72
Operational costs	16	16	20	20	20	52	52
Maintenance costs	16	16	24	24	24	44	44
Total, compressor	60	62	86	86	86	£1.68	£1.68
Wage costs	£2.40	£2.40	£3.60	£2.40	£2.40	£3.60	£2.40
Total costs, £p/h	£3.72	£3.77	£7.36	£4.42	£7.32	£7.60	£6.44
Total costs, £p/m²	37.6	23.2	58.4	22.4	44.2	22.4	16

[handwritten annotations in right margin: 60 ÷ x = 4 ; 1.8 m² ×]

penses for driving the sheeting, extracting the sheeting, transport of equipment and other costs must be included in the calculations. These additional costs can be calculated at 100–150% of the total costs for the equipment (see Table 6.7).

The net costs for driving vertical sheeting (steel sheet piles) in medium hard soil lie in the range of 40p to £1.20/m².

Wage costs are best calculated in terms of hourly pay, and are to be weighed against costs for more mechanised equipment. In this case, wage costs amount to £1.20 per man-hour.

Operational costs include expenses for diesel and lubricating oil consumed. If the compressor is electrically powered, replace the diesel oil costs by those for electricity. With a compressor, operational costs amount to 40–70%.

Estimating for Tractor Shovels

The Clark Equipment Company demonstrate how a customer should be assisted in plant selection, for they appreciate that the wrong choice could make a further sale more difficult. They want, as does any other manufacturer, the customer to have the right machine for the job. They point out that for each application the selection of the right tractor shovel will depend on a combination of some or all of the following factors: (a) tons/yd³/m³ required per hour; (b) operating efficiency; (c) ground conditions; (d) material density; (e) vehicle body or hopper size; (f) cycle length; (g) loading characteristics. Let us examine each of these production factors separately.

(a) *Tons/yd³/m³ required per hour*. With most application studies this item is known and will be given for the basis of calculations, i.e., the contractor will state that output required is 200 tons per hour or 20×9 yd³ or m³ tippers per hour, etc.

(b) *Operating efficiency*. Because of the human element involved in operating a shovel, it is not possible for the machine to be working for 60 minutes in every hour. The driver is inevitably going to stop now and again for a chat, or to light a cigarette, and to work a little slower at the end of the day, etc. It is, then, more practical to estimate production on the basis that the machine will be operating only for 50 minutes in each hour.

This lack of efficiency has one advantage in that it ensures the machine is not being worked continuously at its peak production. No matter how good a machine it is, it will last longer when not worked at its limit.

(c) *Ground conditions*. The most important aspect of ground conditions is to observe whether there is any adverse grade in the cycle. No alterations to production estimates need be made for adverse grades up to 5%, but for each additional 1% grade above this, production estimates should be reduced by 2%. (The operating cycle should be planned where possible to ensure that the downhill section of the cycle be negotiated by the machine when laden, thus virtually eliminating lost time due to the adverse grade.)

Assessing the effect of poor ground, i.e., soft, loose, etc., is solely a matter of experience, but unless visible signs of movement difficulties are apparent, this factor in most cases can be ignored.

(d) *Material density.* The density of the material being handled determines the size of bucket which should be fitted to a particular size of shovel.

(e) *Vehicle body or hopper size.* The size of vehicle body or hopper being loaded, either by volume or external measurement, may affect tractor shovel selection. The following points should be considered:

When loading hoppers: *Lorries*

 (i) Is there adequate boom height and reach to enable easy loading? Ensure that wheels do not have to touch lorry sides in order to evenly distribute load.

 (ii) Is bucket size practical for the lorries being loaded? That is, blade width must be at least 2 ft shorter than the lorry body.

(iii) Preferably not more than 3 buckets to load full payload.

When loading hoppers:

 (i) If loading at cab roof height, ensure bucket length able to fit into hopper.

 (ii) Ensure hopper is able to take several times the bucket capacity.

(f) *Cycle length.* This is the distance travelled during each complete loading operation. All applications must be viewed with the object of reducing the cycle length as much as possible. This can be done by ensuring lorries are correctly positioned when being loaded, that travelling surfaces are kept clean and graded when necessary, and that any unnecessary obstructions are moved.

(g) *Loading characteristics.* Certain materials in stockpile present a considerable resistance when being excavated, e.g., shot rock, iron ore, asphalt, etc. On short cycles this will result in cycle times being extended. Over long cycles, the effect plays a less important part.

When excavating all in bank materials, a similar increase in cycle time must be allowed for.

Calculating Cycle Time

During the first 50 ft of a loading cycle the time will be a constant for each specific model. This constant has been derived by calculation and actual field testing. Times for the following operations include:

bucket loading, back-up from pile, dump and back to pile. *Acceleration and deceleration are included in the constant.*

Up to 2 yd^3	20 sec or 0·333 min
2–6 yd^3	25 sec or 0·416 min
5–9 yd^3	29 sec or 0·480 min
9 yd^3 upwards	33 sec or 0·550 min

In calculating cycle times and production estimating, use hundredths of a minute rather than minutes and seconds. Convert to hundredths of a minute by dividing number of seconds by 60. For example:

$$\frac{sec}{60} = \frac{12}{60} = 0·20 \text{ min}$$

To convert back to seconds simply multiply by 60.

If the cycle distance is over 50 ft by measuring the loader front tyre travelling distance, the average speed both loaded and empty must be determined and the time required for each way added to the constant. For example:

200 ft one-way cycle

Constant for 50 ft	0·333 min
Loaded 150 ft @ 4 m.p.h.	0·425 min
Empty 150 ft @ 6 m.p.h.	0·285 min
Total cycle time	1·043 min

To find the time required to go the 150 ft, use the formula:

$$\frac{\text{Distance}}{\text{m.p.h.} \times 88} = \frac{150}{4 \times 88} = 0·425 \text{ min}$$

The speed was determined with the following rule of thumb:

Loaded m.p.h. — max. first gear speed — 4 m.p.h.
Empty m.p.h. — average between 1st and 2nd gear — 6 m.p.h.

This rule of thumb holds true for smaller machines. Larger machines have progressive shift transmission.

The length of the cycle and the ground condition determine the gear that can be used. Normally the longer the distance, the higher the gear and average speed.

Hourly Owning and Operating Cost Estimate

The following form, which estimates owning and operating costs, is a valuable way of keeping records for any wheeled plant.

Machine:_____   Tyre size:_____

Attachments:_____

_____

List price_____ Bare machine cost, less tyres _____

Hourly Owning Costs
  Depreciation: Bare machine cost
    based on average five years: _____ ÷ 12 000 h_____
  Int., Ins., Taxes:_____ × Del. price ÷ 1000_____

  Total hourly owning cost _____

Hourly Operating Costs
Fuel:
  Diesel Fuel:_____ gal/h × Cost/gal_____ per h
Lubricants: 25% of fuel cost (incl. all
            filters, transm., oil axle lub.,
            grease and hydraulic fluid)   _____ per h

Cutting edge replacement:_____   Est. life_____ h

Tyres replacement cost: _____ Capping cost_____ h

                    Tyre cost per h_____

        Total estimated hourly operating cost_____

Loader Production Estimating

1. *Hopper feeding*—after determining cycle time.
   (*a*) Using specific machine and bucket:

$$\frac{\text{Minutes worked per hour}}{\text{Minutes required per cycle}} \times \frac{\text{Weight of material} \times \text{Bucket size}}{2000} = \text{ton/h}$$

   Example: 55 with $1\frac{1}{2}$ yd^3 bucket; 200 ft cycle as above:

$$\frac{60}{1 \cdot 043} \times \frac{3000 \times 1 \cdot 5}{2000} = 130 \text{ ton/h}$$

(b) To determine the machine size for a job, the production rate required must be known; then estimate the approximate requirement so cycle time can be established. Use this formula:

$$\frac{\text{Minutes per cycle}}{\text{Minutes worked per h}} \times \frac{2000 \times \text{ton/h}}{\text{Material weight}} = \text{Bucket size}$$

Example: 200 ton/h required

$$\frac{1 \cdot 043}{60} \times \frac{2000 \times 200}{3000} = 2 \cdot 3 \text{ yd}^3$$

2. *Loading haul units*—The size of machine and bucket will be determined by the size of the truck. The loader bucket should fill the truck with full bucket loads. In other words, do not select a 2 yd³ bucket for a 5 yd³ truck. Two loads with a $2\frac{1}{2}$ yd³ bucket will just fill the truck. Also the bucket selected must not be longer than the bed of the truck. After determining size of machine, use the following formula:

$$\frac{\text{Truck size}}{\text{Bucket size}} \times \text{Load cycle time} = \text{Time to load truck}$$

Example:

$$\frac{6 \text{ yd}^3 \text{ truck}}{6 \text{ yd}^3 \text{ bucket}} \times 40 \text{ min} = 1 \cdot 2 \text{ min } 1 \text{ truck (or} \times 60 = 72 \text{ sec})$$

To get the hourly capacity in tons per hour:

$$\frac{\text{Minutes worked per hour}}{\text{Minutes per truck}} \times \frac{\text{Material weight} \times \text{Truck size}}{2000}$$

Example:

$$\frac{60}{1 \cdot 2} \times \frac{3000 \times 6}{2000} = 450 \text{ ton/h}$$

To obtain this production there must be enough trucks that the loader does not have to wait.

Bulldozer Operation

With any type of equipment the decision whether to hire or to buy can only be made based on length of use and productivity obtained. Therefore, any information on estimating that productivity factor must be given serious consideration and, because of the wide application of dozing, must be represented here. The Caterpillar Tractor Co. advise that an estimate of bulldozer production can be obtained by using production curves for the bulldozer blade/tractor combination and then applying correction factors.

Production (LCY/h)* = Maximum production × Correction factors

*LCY = loose cubic yards; BCY = bank cubic yards.

The bulldozer production curves give maximum uncorrected production and are based on the following six conditions:

1. 100% efficiency (60 minutes in each hour).
2. Fixed times:
   (a) 0·05 min for power-shift machines.
   (b) 0·1 min for direct-drive machines.
3. Machine cuts for 50 ft, then drifts blade load to dump over a high wall.
4. Soil density of 2300 lb/LCY (3000 lb/BCY). Material swells 30% (load factor of 0·769).
5. Coefficient of traction: Track machines—0·5 or better.
6. Hydraulic blades used.

To obtain estimated production in bank cubic yards, the approximate load factor found in maker's literature should be applied to the corrected production calculated from the formula.

It should be borne in mind that A-blades and cushion blades are not considered production dozing tools. Depending on job conditions, the A-blade and C-blade will average 50–75% of straight-blade production.

An estimated production of a typical 270 hp track-type dozer is given in Figure 6.3.

To calculate an example the following job condition corrections are assumed, utilising a crawler tractor:

Operator	Excellent	1·00
	Average	0·75
	Poor	0–0·60

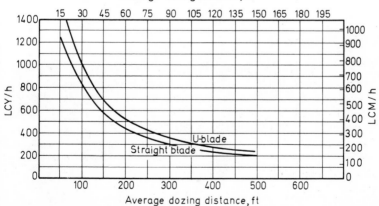

Figure 6.3

Material

1. Weight: correction factor equals 3000 lb/BCY

$$\frac{}{\text{Actual wt/BCY}}$$

or

$$\frac{2300\,\text{lb/LCY}}{\text{Actual wt/LCY}}$$

2. Type:

Loose stockpile	1·20
Hard to cut—frozen*	0·80
Hard to drift—'dead'†	0·80
Rock, ripped or blasted‡	0·60–0·80
Slot dozing	1·20
Visibility: dust, rain, snow, fog or darkness	0·80
Direct-drive transmission	0·80
Blade: light material U-blade (coal)	1·20
blade bowl (stockpiles)	1·30
Job efficiency: 50 min/h	0·84
45 min/h	0·75

Grades:

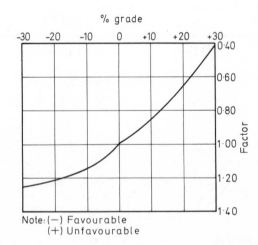

Figure 6.4

*Without tilt cylinder, factor = 0·60; with cable blades = 0·60.
† Dry, non-cohesive material (sand, gravel) or very sticky material.
‡ Factor depends on average rock size and percentage of fines.

For example, to determine average hourly production of the above straight-blade dozer with tilt cyl moving hard-packed clay an average distance of 150 ft down a 15% grade, using a slot-dozing technique, with material weight of 2650 lb/LCY, employing an 'average' operator and job efficiency estimated at 50 min/h, the following calculation may be made:

Uncorrected maximum production: 575 LCY/h (from bulldozer curve).

Applicable correction factors:

Hard-packed clay is 'hard to cut' material	0·80
Grade correction (from Figure 6.4)	1·19
Slot dozing	1·20
Material weight correction	2300–2650
Average operator	0·75
Job efficiency (50 min/h)	0·84

Production = Maximum production × Correction factors
$$= (575 \text{ LCY/h}) (0·80) (1·19) (1·20)$$
$$(2300–2650) \quad (0·75) (0·84)$$
$$= 362 \text{ LCY/h}.$$

Grading

The production of the motor grader (Figure 6.5) is also very important to the contractor for maintenance of haul roads and

Figure 6.5 *Graders are invaluable maids-of-all-work on site, maintaining haul roads, profiling sub-grades and base courses, aligning embankment slopes, etc., but profitability lies in correct cost analysis (courtesy Aveling-Barford Ltd)*

finishing final grades, but its production is subject to many variables. Operator efficiency and the material being worked both influence motor grader production even more than that of other machines. Again quoting Caterpillar's experience, to find the time required to complete a job, the number of passes needed must be known and an estimate of efficiency and average speed must be made:

$$\text{Time in hours} = \frac{(\text{No. of passes})\,(\text{Distance in miles})}{(\text{Average speed, m.p.h.})\,(\text{Eff. factor})}$$

Where average speed is found by this type of calculation:

6 passes @ 3·0 m.p.h. = 18
4 passes @ 4·0 m.p.h. = 16
                        34 total

$$\frac{34}{10} = 3\cdot4 \text{ m.p.h. (average)}$$

For example, to maintain a haul road properly a grader must make one pass in 2nd gear and then two more passes in 3rd gear. How long will it take to complete the job if the haul road is 5·3 miles long?

If 2nd gear speed = 3·5 m.p.h.
and 3rd gear speed = 5·7 m.p.h.
One pass @ 3·5 m.p.h. + two passes @ 5·7 m.p.h.

$$= \text{average speed of } \frac{15\cdot1}{3} = \text{Average speed @ } 5\cdot03 \text{ m.p.h.}$$

$$\text{Time in hours} = \frac{(3 \text{ passes}) \times (5\cdot3 \text{ miles})}{(5\cdot03\,\text{m.p.h.}) \times (0\cdot80\,\text{eff.})} = 3\cdot96 \text{ h}$$

Whenever fill material is used it must be compacted to form a stable base. The number of passes to be made with compacting equipment (Figures 6.6 and 6.7) depends on the material and its moisture content. Specifications for compaction are usually given the contractor by the consulting engineer in terms of Proctor density, modified Proctor or air-void content. Compaction production can be calculated on knowledge of the depth of material and specified number of passes (or this figure may sometimes be the result of trial experimentation).

Caterpillar Tractor Co. suggest the following simplified formula to determine the production for a compactor, with the result expressed in compacted volume per 60 minute hour:

$$\text{Compacted yd}^3/\text{h} = \frac{W \times S \times L \times 16\cdot3}{P}$$

where P = number of machine passes; W = compacted width, ft/pass; S = average speed, in m.p.h.; L = lift thickness in compacted inches; 16·3 = conversion constant.

Figure 6.6. *A method of applying compaction by using two vibrating rollers operated in tandem, on the site of the M62 trans-Pennine motorway (courtesy Stothert and Pitt Ltd.)*

122

Figure 6.7. *Two vibrating rollers having individual tractor units for their work of compacting colliery waste on a landscaping contract (courtesy Stothert and Pitt Ltd.)*

Bank state production can be estimated by allowing for shrinkage. The following average speeds of compaction equipment may be used as guidelines when actual speed measurements are not available:

Self-propelled sheepsfoot, 5 m.p.h.
Self-propelled tamping foot, 6 m.p.h.
Self-propelled pneumatic, 7 m.p.h.
Sheepsfoot and tamping rollers towed
   by a wheel tractor, 5–10 m.p.h.
Sheepsfoot and tamping rollers towed
   by TTT 3–4 m.p.h.
Towed pneumatic rollers 3–5 m.p.h.
Grid rollers towed by motor grader, 12 m.p.h.
800 series compactors, 5–9 m.p.h.

CHAPTER SEVEN

Methods of Plant Selection and Costing Procedures

Plant selection is often dictated by the very nature of the contract and in many instances is written into the contract documents by the consulting engineer; therefore, the successful contractor has to be prepared to plant a job, either from his own holding or alternatively by purchasing new plant or hiring in from specialist and other plant hirers. The latter industry has gained in strength purely from a financial aspect.

The main factor being 'maintenance costs', the variables between company-owned plant and that of a hire company are as follows:

1. Damage is charged for. When a hire company has this contingent written into a hire contract, the contractor has to stand his own damage costs, unless he insures against them and that is expensive too.
2. Plant tends to be purchased on its maintenance record and not on maximum performance or slick salesmen's gimmicks.
3. Plant is sold off before a major expansion and overhaul becomes necessary. A hire company often has a secondary organisation dealing with the disposal of redundant plant.
4. A hire company will carry out maintenance on a piecemeal basis as opposed to a centralised maintenance depot. A great many contracting companies have in the past built up large works departments with all the profit-absorbing costs, but there is a greater tendency today to localise maintenance by mobile staff and facilities. The basic difference is that the contractor treats maintenance as a service, whereas to a plant hirer it is a cost.

Depreciation percentages are another financial aspect. In the latter years these have fallen appreciably due to the influence of the following points:

1. Plant hirers purchase to a programme, not individual demand.
2. The plant-hire company, with its disposal department, sells off its redundant plant at advantageous prices—the contractor is not as demanding. Then the plant-hire company, purchasing in numbers rather than the occasional machine, has very definite advantages of negotiating a much more lucrative deal with the manufacturer under a buy-back arrangement.
3. Again, a plant-hire company in the UK, with the Government operating an investment grant scheme (which was in effect for many years), tends to work on a three- to four-year cycle of plant replacement. This obviates the critical period in the life of a piece of plant when it is reaching the time for a major overhaul, particularly so if the machine has been double-shifted on heavy excavation work, which often happens in Britain due to time loss through bad weather conditions. It also ensures he has up-to-date plant. The contractor either cannot or does not consider it necessary to make an item of plant redundant just for the privilege of owning an up-to-date machine.

Operating costs are not only influenced by maintenance. Operators play a most important role. The contractor is usually short of reliable plant operators, whereas the plant hirer can keep his team more fully employed and usually on one type of machine. By allocating a machine to an operator as his *personal* piece of plant he ensures a larger production output and the man takes a pride in keeping his machine up to a good standard of efficiency. An example could be equipment such as that shown in Figure 7.1. All three parties benefit: the company employing the plant hirer, the plant hirer and the operator.

A plant hirer must have a commercial mind equally as much as a practical mind when considering his plant-holding potential. A plant-hire business cannot be successful without a proper knowledge of modern financial machinery. The company should have the know-how of the optimum size of its undertaking. This has to be carefully calculated bearing in mind location and costing of overheads. It is more or less accepted that a plant holding of less than £250 000 at original cost is not likely to be very efficient.

There are many theories of when to sell off plant, but a good rule-of-thumb calculation is: sell when the annual increase in maintenance costs exceeds the annual decrease in depreciation plus interest costs. More sophisticated systems are applied based on averages, where depreciation costs are high in the first year's life of a piece of plant. Timing for selling must be flexible; basically a plant-hire owner should be prepared to sell equipment at any time, provided the price is sufficient to show a useful net profit. The position is influenced with Government grants and what a company has laid down in the way of policy.

Depreciation of plant is a controversial subject; it varies with a lot of companies, but a good yardstick is the Inland Revenue System. After all, it is the only one recognised by the Government and therefore should be universally adopted by industry. Company accountants, naturally, have to be guided by the board of directors and

Figure 7.1 *Excavating rock on the E4 highway at Granna, in Sweden, using a Caterpillar 994—an example of the larger size of mobile equipment available to contractors*

therefore there is a variety of results in trading figures spread over the UK plant-hire industry.

The actual life of plant is limited by many factors. After a period of years, a major part can give trouble and it will be cheaper to replace than to repair. Some machines appear to wear out quicker than others and this entails costly maintenance figures. Maintenance expenditure is one of the main costs of a plant-hiring company and includes: labour and materials in the workshop, proportion of overheads and downtime and lack of earning revenue.

To indicate a reasonable suggested depreciation formula we give the following list of percentages:

1. Cranes over 50 tons should be depreciated at $7\frac{1}{2}\%$ straightline. After three years the crane will be written down to 62% of the

original cost. A sale at this time is most unlikely and after ten years it will be 20% of the original cost.

2. Cranes between 10 and 50 tons should be depreciated at $12\frac{1}{2}\%$ reducing. After three years the written-down value is 54% of the original cost.

3. Smaller telescopic cranes, large earthmoving equipment and compressors should be written down by $16\frac{2}{3}\%$ reducing. After three years it will be about $46\frac{1}{2}\%$.

4. Tractor shovels, road rollers, etc., should be written off on a 20% reducing basis. After three years the written down cost will be just under 41%.

5. Excavators, smaller tractor shovels, fork-lift trucks and large dumpers (especially where there is no buy-back) should be written off at 25% reducing. After three years this will mean that book cost is less than 34%.

6. Dumpers, small cranes and other smaller pieces of equipment, especially where there is very little of a second-hand market, should be written off at $33\frac{1}{3}\%$ reducing. After three years, the equipment will be down to less than 24%.

7. If, at any time, equipment is becoming obsolete (such as un-silenced compressors) there should be a special extra write down to adjust the book value with the second-hand market.

The plant-hire industry in the UK today, particularly the successful companies, negotiate a 'buy-back' contract with the manufacturers of plant. When this was coupled with the Government investment grant (which no longer applies) it gave them, as near as possible, working cost figures for whatever period they opted to keep their plant. Naturally, like all business, there are the exceptions, where machinery is fickle and does not follow the general and known pattern, but by and large the scheme is pretty foolproof.

A buy-back is a guaranteed trade-in price for a piece of equipment after a given period of time and it is effectively a warranty of the second-hand value. This works conversely with the purchase of a new piece of plant, where the vendor quotes a warranty for a given period of time against the failure of the machine subject to fair wear and tear. The purchaser is equally bound to see that the machine receives proper attention, maintenance and repairs, during the period of time he keeps the machine and for which the buy-back price is calculated.

The arrangements between manufacturer and purchaser vary to some extent but generally one finds that after a nominal period of use the maker guarantees the purchaser a predetermined percentage of the original price paid, on the understanding that if the purchaser wishes he is at liberty to retail the machine to another source if the price is more to his advantage. As a rule the agreement is dependent on a limited number of hours' use and plant must be in good condition when surrendered. In particular, the engine must be in good shape and certain specified parts must not show excessive wear. One way these conditions are enforced is for the manufacturer's service team to make periodic inspections, and the user is responsible for this expense.

Stringent though these conditions may seem, they work to the general benefit. From the user's point of view he knows his working costs to a fine degree (an essential in these days of fierce competition) and clears uncertainty from his calculations and it keeps depreciation to a minimum. But best of all, it guarantees plant in good condition being turned back into the second-hand market.

Much second-hand equipment goes into the home market but a great deal, probably the majority, goes overseas. So these conditions serve to establish standards of international acceptability and ensure one of the essential aspects of making this buy-back system work by virtually insisting that the vendors have a proper sales organisation. As with any section of the construction business, the obvious essential is that the contractor has the safeguard of dealing with a reputable organisation, whether manufacturer, agent or distributor, to give him the necessary after-sales service. The organisation must be 100 per cent good. The buy-back is only as good as the vendor who negotiates it and therefore the purchaser must be sure and certain in his own mind that in three years, or whatever time has been prescribed, the vendor will be able to honour the contract. The purchaser, too, has to honour his part of the contract in the same spirit and he has a bounden duty to ensure that the machine is in no way abused or neglected. Buy-backs are a warranty of the second-hand value and not an opportunity to make money out of the vendor.

This is a system which is growing in popularity in the UK but naturally it is only operating where business is repetitive and on a reasonably large scale. Again this is an aspect of business that is very little known or understood on the European continent. They just do not believe it can work. But work it does—and soon American- and Canadian-influenced companies, with continental offshoots or daughter companies, will force the local competition to follow suit.

Costing Control Procedures

In this section it is proposed to give a general costing control procedure, including the reason for this method of control, together with budgetary control, periodic operating statement, budgetary control schedule, monthly operating and thirteen-monthly operating statements. No business activity will flourish unless a strict financial procedure is inaugurated at the commencement of operations. To this end we wish to include the basic practices to produce a yearly financial statement.

The most important advantages to be derived from the utilisation of control procedures are that they (a) clarify and define all instructions, (b) provide a reference back on all matters of procedure, (c) improve administrative and executive control, (d) facilitate the teaching of staff, (e) eliminate confusion and dispute on matters of procedure, duties and responsibilities, (f) relieve management of the need to repeat instructions on routine matters, (g) provide better co-ordination between individuals and departments, (h) ensure more uniform results and facilitate the measurement of operation and performance.

The control authority through whom all directives and policies are issued in the form of control procedures is the managing director, who has the authority to approve by his signature or reject all proposed procedures.

Financial Planning and Budgetary Control

Budgetary control is a management technique and its objectives are:

1. To plan and control the income and expenditure of a business so that the maximum profit is obtained.
2. To plan and control the financing of the business operations so that adequate working capital is available for carrying out the policy dictated by the management.
3. To plan and control the financing of the business expenditure and relate this to the earning capacity of the company.
4. To reveal the extent by which actual results have exceeded or failed to reach the target budget set; and so to establish the causes of variation as a basis for corrective action by management.
5. To make the most economical use of the assets and trading capacity of a company.

A budget is the estimate of future trading activity expressed in financial terms. Its purpose is to provide standards of expected performance against which actual results can be measured.

The budget will cover a period of one year forward and will be divided into 13 monthly accounting periods. Thus the internal accounting system will be geared to produce the required information at the end of each periodic accounting period.

The control of profit and expenditure is achieved by setting and maintaining financial operating standards to cover every aspect of a company's operations.

Like all standards, these are instruments of measurement only. Once these have been set, they become less important than the variations that are disclosed when comparisons are made between the standard set and actual performance achieved. Moreover, they are not permanent. General economic conditions may change, prime cost elements such as wages, materials, etc., may be affected by national policies or negotiated agreements.

Because the budget is the estimate of future trading activity, it follows that a periodic revision of the target it contains will be necessary to reflect changes in trading conditions; for example: (a) permanent changes in the type of work undertaken, or whenever entry into a new field is planned; (b) following upon the provision of additional facilities either, for example, in staff, plant or workshop facilities; (c) to reflect changes in elements of costs over which management has no control, e.g. variations in the buying prices of the product used in the operations, national or regional wages, new increases in National Insurance contributions, etc., or other Government imposts; (d) when it becomes necessary to revise budgets that may have proved erroneous in the light of user experience.

In these circumstances the standards set will have to be reconsidered and perhaps reset. As a result, fresh schedules will have to be compiled altering the various units of measurement, so that they will at all times provide an authoritative and current reference on all matters relating to budgetary control.

Fundamental Requirements

There are a number of prerequisites for the successful operation of budgetary control. These are: (a) well-defined lines of authority; (b) the acceptance of senior staff, and other key personnel, of the responsibility for controlling their department's expenditure; (c) adequate accounting and statistical records; (d) intelligent forecasting and anticipation; (e) the co-operation of all personnel; (f) the *determination of management to make the system work*.

Common Terms Used

Profitability—The measure of the efficiency by which any business is conducted is the level of profit obtained.

Activity level—This is the actual figure of sales to turnover achieved either on an annual or periodic basis. The norm or budget is expressed as 100% and the actual sales achieved is expressed as a percentage of the norm or budget set.

Fixed expenses—Those which are constant for the trading year at all levels of activity irrespective of changes in the volume of work undertaken, e.g. directors' remuneration, office salaries, rent, rates, accountancy fees, hire-purchase charges, general insurance, depreciation charges.

Variable expenses—Costs or expenses which vary in direct proportion to the value of work done, e.g. direct wages which are aligned to piecework reimbursement. Material usage which is constant to the value produced.

Semi-variable expenses—Costs or expenses which vary with the value of sales achieved, but not in direct proportion thereto, e.g. postage, stationery, advertising, transport expenses, services, etc.

Controllable expenses—Certain categories of expenses are either wholly or partly controlled by reasons of economy in consumption or use, e.g. electricity, consumable stores, and also other prime costs depending on efficient labour utilisation and adequate allocation of resources.

Non-controllable expenses—These are fixed costs and charges or expenses arising from external factors over which management can exercise no direct influence, e.g. purchasing costs—generally payments to nominated sub-contractors and suppliers—fixed charges such as rates, loan or hire-purchase interest charges.

Gross profit margins—These are influenced by the degree of management control exerted over production operating costs and also by the estimating and pricing policy in use by the company.

Net profit margins—These are influenced to a marked degree by management's control over the general administration overhead expenses incurred in operating the company's activities.

Budgetary Control and Periodic Operating Statement

In this section we examine the different functions of budgetary control and the periodic operating statement and show how they are integrated into a common management control system in the specific areas of profits, costs and expenses.

The following two accounting schedules contribute substantially to management control of profit and expense:

1. The budget, as defined on the previous pages, is a forecast of the pattern of sales, costs and expenses for the year ahead. It is con-

structed bearing in mind past performance, knowledge of current events and trends and a company's future plans and policy. Naturally, as the forward picture changes, the budget may have to be revised and brought into line with the situation created.
2. Monthly operating statement covering a period of $\frac{1}{13}$ of the year (i.e. 4 weeks) shows the income from sales/work done, the operating costs in achieving those sales, gross profit, indirect overheads and operating profit secured.

The operating costs are set out in the same format as the budget. The operating statement is a columnal profit and loss account which excludes sundry income and profits and losses not arising from actual operating activity. It shows the budget and actual revenue and expenditure for the period under review and also a most important factor, the variations between the two.

Examples of Variation from Budget

A budget variation is the difference between the amount of budget permissible expenditure and the actual amount spent in each category of expense. On the income side this is the difference between the target set of actual sales and work done or sales achieved.

The operating statement is so designed that the variations and the trends are readily seen. Therefore, from the examination of the periodic operating statement, management will identify the variations and, if significant, will seek the cause, find a solution and ensure that remedial action is taken.

Variations from the budget in respect of the incurred cost of sales (that is the direct/prime costs) should be carefully analysed to determine whether they are due to: (*a*) increased turnover, (*b*) higher material costs, (*c*) less efficient utilisation of materials and labour, (*d*) increase of labour charges.

Master Budgetary Control Schedule

The board of directors in conjunction with the chief accountant set targets for future operations of the business, to scrutinise all results and comparative operating statements and to take or initiate action, as shown by those results, to be necessary.

It is the responsibility of the accountant to maintain the present operating schedule and, when necessary, following a discussion with the board of directors, to recalculate the standards. The circulation of this control procedure and the schedules attached to it are restricted to the board of directors and the accountant.

Further responsibilities of the accountant are to keep accurately all records needed for the prompt preparation of the comparative operating statements, to assist in taking action decided upon by the board of directors, and to report back on such happenings affecting the targets shown on the schedule. The schedules are composed of a series of targets from which can be measured the results of actual performance.

Occasionally, certain changes in the business necessitate changes in the standard, but it must be remembered that the figures laid down are based on the predetermination of results. To enable the necessary application of close control in respect of expenditure, the budgetary control schedules can be reduced to 4-week operating figures.

The annual totals of forecast expenditure, the 'norm', column 2 of the schedule, is divided into 13 to give the norm or 100% for each operating period.

It is impossible to state exactly what the sales are likely to be for any one month, therefore the control schedules should be projected and designed to cover activity levels at 60, 70, 80, 90, 110, 120, 130, 140, and 150%, respectively, of the 100% norm activity.

For each level of sales volume achieved, there is a predetermined level of expense and above all a predetermined level of profit. By controlling expenses at the required level, as indicated in a budget, the planned profit should be achieved. The build up of the schedules is such that each expense is shown in its proper order.

The costs fall into two categories, namely the direct cost (cost of sales) and the overhead charges. The prime costs, referred to as B, or the schedules when deducted from the value of sales A, produce a resultant figure, C, known as the gross operating profit. Following this are itemised the other administration expenses analysed into sections, i.e. property expenses, general administration charges, selling expenses, finance expenses and depreciation charges. The above expenses totalled are deducted from the gross operating profit C which produces the operating profit (before tax, etc.).

Items of capital expenditure (such as new plant) are *not* included as operating expenses. For example, plant and equipment may be purchased, through hire-purchase facilities, in the periodic payment, usually by banker's standing order; this payment includes the re-payment of the capital sum involved in the purchase of the new asset together with the interest to be repaid on the capital sum originally borrowed from a finance house. It is only the interest charge in servicing the loan which should be charged as an administrative expense. This interest charge may be identified from a scrutiny of the hire-purchase contract agreement.

In the circumstances, when leasing vehicles or plant is considered, the total charges are recoverable in the company's administration overheads, because the vehicles or plant are leased or hired, belong to the leasing company, and do not increase the assets of a company.

The operating profit/loss disclosed in the budgeting control schedules should not be confused with the trading profit and loss account produced by a company's auditors. Often these prepared accounts will show other sources of revenue, e.g. interest in bank deposits, income from property renting, etc., which have no direct relationship to the operating control schedules, which confine themselves to actual and budget expenses incurred in achieving a certain volume of sales or turnover.

These operating schedules provide the means of direct comparison and control. Individual variations can be seen and management are enabled to take action on those results disclosed.

The Preparation of the Monthly Operating Statement

It is the prerogative of the company financial controller, assisted by the accountant, to prepare the periodic operating statement for discussion by the executive directors at a period following the end of the month under review. Monthly operating statements should be prepared for each month's trading, showing the trading figures for the current month and the cumulative figure for the year to date.

The procedure of control is based upon the principle of the comparisons of standards, i.e. the budget with the actual incurred expenditure for any given or attained sales level (the activity level), action being taken to correct any excessive variation from the budget or standard having established the reason for the variation.

The budget on permissible expenses gives those shown and listed on the master budgetary control schedule for the activity level achieved and these are entered directly on the monthly operating statement.

Actual expenses are those incurred according to the books of the company, e.g. purchases ledger, sales ledger, salaries and wages ledger, etc. Variation is the difference between the permissible and actual figures, whether plus or minus.

Each month it is necessary to establish the total sales and, by the use of the 1% interpolation figure, it is possible to determine the activity level.

Example

The 4-week target 'norm' of 'sales/work done' at 100% activity is £15 000. Therefore, 1% is £15 000 divided by 100=£150.

If the value of sales/work done for the period is established at, say, £13 500, what is the activity level?

£13 500 ÷ £150 = Percentage activity level=90%

Therefore, use 90% as the activity level.

This method of interpolation can be applied to both variable and semi-variable expenses. *Note*: fixed expenses are not interpolated.

Schedule X, Part I (see overleaf)

Item (*a*). Enter the budget figure of . . .

Item *A* or (*b*). Enter the total sales/work done value.

Item (*c*). Enter the variation between actual and standard whether this be plus or minus.

Item (*d*). Compute the activity level as described earlier in the control procedure.

Schedule X, Part II (see overleaf)

In the budget expenses, listed in column (*I*), enter all the permissible expenses interpolated as necessary in accordance with the appropriate level of activity determined, i.e. column (*d*) as above. In the actual expenses column (*K*) insert the incurred costs taken from the books of accounts.

Variation

Deduct actual expenses incurred and entered in column (*K*) from the budget entries appearing in column (*f*) and enter the resultant figure in the variation column (*L*) or (*M*). Where the budget figure is above the actual expense entry, the difference is a saving and is entered in the minus column as less expense has been incurred; if the actual entry is greater than the budget figure, the difference is an excess and is entered in the plus column. Entries made in the minus column should be recorded in black; excess or plus column entries (*L*) or (*M*) should be entered in red.

By reference to the previous month's comparative operating statements, the cumulative variations year to date are obtained by addition and inserted in the appropriate columns (*N*) or (*O*). Complete the expenses to date columns (*P*) and (*Q*) by bringing forward the totals of the previous month's operating statements.

Schedule X. THE MASTER PERIODIC OPERATING STATEMENT

PART I

(a)	Budget forecast income from work done	£	
(b)A	Actual sales income from work done	£	
(c)	Variation—actual from budget [col. (a) minus col. (b)]	= £	+ or −
(d)	Actual sales income (col. A) expressed as a % of budget forecast [col. (a)]	=	%

PART III

(e)	Budget forecast income for year to date	+ £	
(f)	Actual sales income for year to date	= £	
(g)	Variation year to date of actual income from budget forecast [col. (e) minus col. (f)]	= £	+ or −
(h)	Actual sales income to date expressed as a % of budget forecast [col. (e)]	=	%

PART II

Code reference	Item	Expenses		Variation				Expenses to date	
				This period		Year to date			
		Budget	Actual	plus	minus	plus	minus	Budget	Actual
	(I)	(J)	(K)	(L)	(M)	(N)	(O)	(P)	(Q)
1	Cost of hire sub-contract machines								
2	Cost of leasing machines								
3	Cost of fuel and oil								
4	Road fund licences								
5	Insurance of machines								
6	Drivers, gross wages (including employers' N.H.I., less S.E.T. plus graduated pension)								
7	Maintenance cost of materials used, e.g. spares, accessories, tyres, etc.								

PART II—continued

8	Maintenance section gross wages, etc.						
9	Drivers' subsistence expenses						
B	Total prime costs						
C	Gross operating profit (col. A minus col. B)	—	—	—	—	—	—
	Gross operating profit as a % of sales (col. A)	—	—	—	—	—	—
	Overhead Expenses Property expenses						
	Administration salaries						
	General administration expenses						
	Selling expenses						
	Finance expenses						
	Depreciation						
D	Total administration expenses						
E	Operating profit pre-tax, etc. (col. C minus col. D)	—	—	—	—	—	—
	Operating profit as a % of sales (A)	—	—	—	—	—	—
	Remarks						

Action

Schedule X, Part III

Complete this section, which is the cumulative totals of previous operating statements plus the current month's figures. Note that item (*h*), % of budget forecast, has to be calculated from the ratio that the total figure in column (*f*) bears to column (*e*).

The principal objective of these periodic operating statements, which are an integral part of financial management control, is to ensure that given an adequate volume of work a company earns a satisfactory profit on its operations to reward shareholders and finance expansion.

The periodic operating statement highlights factors adversely affecting profitability. Management must take action early and be decisive enough to correct these factors and so maximise the profit return by lifting the overall level of efficiency.

In reading the net operating profit figure on the operating statement, this must be done in conjunction with the overall variation figure so that any excess, due to prepayment, is allowed for in establishing the final profit (pre-tax, etc.) for the period under review.

Interpretation of Results

One of the most important duties of management is the interpretation of results. The first exercise is a complete study of the variations, and the reasons for the variations, and evaluating what the effect of these has been and will be on a company. From these findings, management will have to decide what action has to be taken, when and by whom that action will have to be implemented. The reasons for the variations may be obscure but management nevertheless must endeavour to find the root cause. All the statistical data presented must be compared. Trends are important in the construction industry. The present trend is definitely for the more employment of the plant-hire section. In the past it has always been a prestige evaluation to have one's own large and expensive plant depot, but with the escalation of labour rates and governmental taxation, particularly Selective Employment Tax, it has led many companies to drop the expensive plant depot set-up and turn to contract hire for small and large high-valued units. So from a previous year's working and trade figure to the following year, with the change in policy, there can be a vast amount of variation and it will have to be allowed to settle down and then be evaluated, probably after the second year's working.

Historic statistics are of little value unless action is taken to correct variations from standard or the control figure established. They can only give an indication as to the amount of correction necessary, but it must be appreciated that the recovery of yesterday's loss is problematical.

Basically, if a loss calls for an extra effort, that effort used to control the loss should have been used to produce an extra profit. Control can be applied by setting standards and targets for the future. Management setting these standards must do so, with the effort being borne in mind, and temper the required effort with reality. Should an expense be £1000 overspent and the normal forecast be £1500 in the coming month, it is bad policy to state that this expense must only be allowable at £500 in the coming month and hope that in this way the £1000 excess of expenditure will be recovered. In effect, management would be saying that the expense can be permitted at one-third of the cost.

Applying this analogy to materials could operate correctly with only one-third of its required materials. One thousand pounds might not possibly be recovered in one month, but it could be recovered over a three-month period without embarrassment. The effort then put in may give a bigger recovery because the target recovery rate set is achieved. Forecasting is an art which only comes with practice— a good rule is to aim above the norm expected, but below the maximum achievable.

Company employees, particularly on the management side, should know what the aims of the business are, whether this applies to one particular department or the policy of the company as a whole. For this reason, it is important that departmental heads should attend regular meetings convened by the managing director. They can be at weekly or monthly intervals dependent on the topic to be discussed.

The 'decision factor' is responsible for a great many eruptions in business life. It is the ability to make a decision—to say 'Yes' or 'No' is far better than no decision. If it is shown to be wrong at a later stage then it does allow for the correct decision to be made on the next occasion.

Monthly Financial Report

It is the prerogative of the accounts department, under the direction of the chief accountant, to prepare a relevant financial report for the attention of the managing director not later than one week after the end of the monthly accounting period under review. Referring to the chart overleaf:

The Monthly Financial Report

Income (1)	£	p	Payments made (2)	£	p	Credits outstanding (3)	£	p	Debits outstanding (4)	£	p	Cash book reconciliation (5)	£	p
As per sales ledger			Wages			Against invoices			Over 5 months old			Bank deposits		
Per contract hire			Salaries			Others			Over 4 months old			Bank withdrawals In cash By cheque payment		
Other income (e.g., S.E.T., refund, etc.)			Per standing orders						Over 3 months old					
			Per invoices						Over 2 months old			Balance as per bank statement		
			Inland revenue						Up to 2 months old					
			Ministry of Social Security									Balance as per cash book reconciliation		
			Others											
Totals														

Remarks

Income—column (1)

Enter the income from:

(*a*) Sales as per sales ledger.

(*b*) Income from contract hire.

(*c*) Other income, e.g. investments, rents, tax refunds, etc.

Expenditure—column (2)

(*a*) Salaries and wages.

(*b*) Standing orders.

(*c*) Purchase ledger.

(*d*) Inland revenue.

(*e*) Ministry of Social Security, etc.

Credits outstanding—column (3)

(*a*) Outstanding payments, etc.

Debits outstanding—column (4)

(*a*) Enter cash accounts analysed into the duration time limit of the debt.

(*b*) This column of entries is most important as it indicates to management whether the credit control is effective or otherwise.

Cash book reconciliation—column (5)

(*a*) Bank lodgements.

(*b*) Bank withdrawals, representing cheques drawn in respect of salaries/wages, N.H.I. stamps, petty cash or float. Payment of invoices, P.A.Y.E.

(*c*) Bank balance as per bank statement.

(*d*) Bank balance as per cash book reconciliation.

Cash Book Reconciliation—Bank Balance

This column is completed at the end of the four-weekly accounting period. At the end of this period total up the entries in columns (1) to (4) and pencil in total figures.

Refer to bank statement and, using the stubs of the cheque book, tick off the drawn cheques which appear as passing through the accounts for payment in the debit column of the bank statement. Total up the cheques which have been drawn but not yet passed into the bank for payment.

Thus, the balance shown by the bank statement is not the true financial position, because inevitably there will be cheques drawn for payment of an account which have not been presented by the payee, or cash and cheques received by a company and not credited to their bank accounts.

The cash book is the barometer of a company's financial position and is the heart of any accounting system.

General Liquidity

A company must not just plan for profit making, cash flow must also be watched very carefully, for without cash it is impossible to meet the day-to-day requirements, particularly to meet salaries/wages, repayment of loans, interest payments, inland revenue and dividend payments. It will not maintain these payments for long unless it is profitable. Business with good profit records have been in trouble by over-stretching their financial resources and thus being unable to meet essential commitments.

Calculating a Hire Rate

To enable a factual hire rate to be calculated, the constituents of the overall operating cost are shown graphically in Figure 7.2. The cost is plotted vertically, the horizontal ordinate being a time base. The time base is interpretable in two ways, in calendar years and in working hours. The rate of expenditure is recouping capital cost depreciation and interest is strictly related to calendar time, whereas expenditure in maintenance, etc., is substantially related to working hours. Before a hire rate can be calculated, the relation between working hours and calendar time has to be established. This is the utilisation factor. Once the average utilisation throughout the life of a machine has been assessed then the maintenance cost and capital charges can be plotted to the same time scale as on the diagrams.

Capital charges are represented by Figure 7.2(a), which shows the recoupment of the total initial purchase cost, less sale value, plus interest. It will be noted that, for the purpose of costing, a regular depreciation rate on a straight-line basis has been taken, so that a constant hire rate throughout the useful life of the machine can be established. It is recognised, of course, that the disposal market for used plant depreciates values much more rapidly in the early years, but provided the original assessment is reasonably accurate, then the depreciated value should accord with the market disposal value at the appropriate time. The effect of interest payments at a fixed rate on a reducing capital value is to slightly deflect the depreciation line as shown.

A typical characteristic for maintenance expenditure is shown in Figure 7.2(b), which indicates a steadily rising pattern of total maintenance expenditure with working hours. The vertical steps in the characteristic at X and Y represent expenditure in depot overhauls. All costs of spares fitted both on site and in depot overhauls, labour, and establishment charges are included.

143

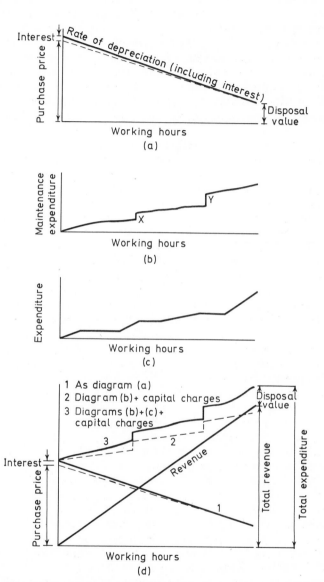

Figure 7.2. *Constituents of total machine operating cost: (a) capital charges; (b) maintenance expenditure; (c) cost of insurance, licensing, etc; (d) total machine operating cost*

There are usually some heads of expenditure which are fixed without reference to a particular time base and typical of these are insurance, licensing for road use, etc. The cumulative cost of these is shown in Figure 7.2(c).

Figures 7.2(a)–(c) show the constituents which, when aggregated, plot the relationship between total machine operating costs (including financial, fixed, and maintenance charges but not consumable items such as fuel and lubricants) and working hours. The resulting addition produces Figure 7.2(d), to which has been added a revenue line which shows the average rate at which income has to be earned relative to working hours to recoup bare operating costs. For simplicity, the effect of taxation concessions has not been included in the diagrams, and any profit element will, of course, have to be added to the 'break-down' revenue line. Thus an hourly, daily, or weekly hire rate may be calculated, which is equally economic to both owner and user.

Table 7.1 shows the proportional effect on the average annual cost of changing the value of some of the main constituents of total cost. Data in accordance with a typical situation is set out in column (1) for retention periods up to 10 years. The effect of progressively changing one factor only by the proportion indicated at the head of each column is set out in columns (2)–(17).

The minimum cost attained in column (1), for a retention period of six years, is taken as unity and all other costs in the table are relative to this.

The existing data on which column (1) has been calculated is as follows:

Disposal price, P
Investment allowance, 30% of purchase price
Initial allowance, 10% of purchase price
Annual allowance, 25% of the written-down value
Standard rate of tax, 39p in the £ ⎱ total £0·538
Profits tax   15p in the £ ⎰ total £0·538
Interest rate, 6% per annum
Breakdown time, T

Capital and Operating Costs of Excavating Machines

The analysis in Table 7.2 may seem novel in some respects but it is useful in the sense that, knowing the output required or the bucket capacity required to achieve an output, some indication can be gained from the rule-of-thumb figures of the capital cost involved. To be fair to certain manufacturers of hydraulic excavators, a separate

Table 7.1. EFFECT OF CHANGES IN COST FACTORS ON ECONOMIC RETENTION PERIOD FOR $\frac{3}{4}$ YD^3 EXCAVATORS

Period of retention (years)	Current factors	Resale prices			Breakdown				Investment allowance			Purchase price		Rate of tax			Interest rate
		0·7P	0·65P	0·4P	0·6T	0·5T	0·3T	0·25T	25%	20%	0%	Plus 10%	Less 10%	0·6 in £	0·575 in £	0·45 in £	7%
(1)	(1)	(2)	(3)	(4)	(5)	(6)	(7)	(8)	(9)	(10)	(11)	(12)	(13)	(14)	(15)	(16)	(17)
1	3·82	2·96	3·12	4·24	3·83	3·83	3·81	3·81	3·79	3·79	3·82	4·24	3·40	3·40	3·53	4·41	3·89
2	2·20	1·82	2·00	2·39	2·23	2·22	2·19	2·19	2·17	2·18	2·26	2·42	1·99	1·97	2·04	2·53	2·25
3	1·13	0·91	1·02	1·25	1·17	1·15	1·13	1·12	1·19	1·30	1·74	1·24	1·03	0·90	0·97	1·46	1·19
4	1·05	0·91	0·98	1·14	1·10	1·12	1·04	1·03	1·08	1·15	1·50	1·13	0·97	0·86	0·92	1·32	1·10
5	1·01	0·92	0·97	1·08	1·07	1·05	1·00	0·98	1·03	1·08	1·38	1·08	0·94	0·85	0·89	1·25	1·05
6	1·00	0·94	0·98	1·06	1·07	1·05	0·98	0·97	1·00	1·05	1·30	1·06	0·94	0·86	0·89	1·22	1·04
7	1·01	0·97	1·00	1·06	1·08	1·06	0·99	0·97	1·00	1·04	1·26	1·05	0·95	0·87	0·90	1·21	1·04
8	1·02	1·00	1·03	1·07	1·12	1·07	1·00	0·98	1·01	1·04	1·25	1·06	0·97	0·89	0·92	1·22	1·05
9	1·04	1·04	1·06	1·09	1·15	1·10	1·02	1·00	1·02	1·06	1·24	1·08	1·00	0·93	0·94	1·23	1·06
10	1·06	1·08	1·09	1·12	1·18	1·13	1·05	1·02	1·04	1·07	1·25	1·10	1·03	0·96	0·97	1·26	1·07

Note: The minimum cost for each condition in the table is underlined.

column has been included to show the cost saving which can be made if one is prepared to accept the 'unconventional'.

Ownership Costs

This amount is the sum of the hourly charges for depreciation and a figure to cover interest charges, tax and insurance.

Table 7.2. COST ANALYSIS FOR EXCAVATING MACHINERY

Faceshovel bucket capacity	Cost of conventional faceshovel	Cost of conventional hydraulic excavator	Cost of unconventional hydraulic excavator	Rubber-tyred shovel capacity	Cost of rubber-tyred shovel
m^3 (yd^3) £	£	£	£	m^3 (yd^3) £	£
1 (1¼)	17 000	14 000	9 300	2 (2½)	13 000
1½ (2)	27 500	26 000		3 (4)	24 500
2½ (3¼)	45 000	50 000	23 000	4½ (6)	35 000
3¼ (4¼)	51 000			7½ (10)	63 500
Rule-of-thumb estimates					
Cost/lb of machine weight	24p	40p	35–50p	—	55p
Cost/yd^3 of bucket capacity	£13 000	£14 000	£7 500	—	£6 000

On rubber-tyred shovels the hourly depreciation charge is calculated by dividing the delivered price of the machine (less the cost of the tyres which appear as a 'consumable' in operating costs) by the depreciation period in hours. This system uses the straight-line 'write-off' method and does not allow for resale value or salvage value of the machine. This method is not entirely satisfactory since all machines must have some residual value, but the practice has gained favour since the value of used equipment is not stable. The useful life of a machine is also difficult to determine since it will depend

Table 7.3. ESTIMATED LIFE OF EXCAVATING MACHINERY

Bucket capacity yd^3	Faceshovel		Dragline	
	years	hours	years	hours
⅜–¾	5	10 000	5	10 000
1–1½	6	12 000	9	18 000
2 and over	8	16 000	12	24 000

to a large extent on the nature of the task and the standard of maintenance. A generally accepted depreciation period for rubber-tyred shovels is 10 000 h, although in hard rock applications, 6000 h for both rubber-tyred shovels and hydraulic excavators would seem

Table 7.4 OPERATING COSTS FOR VERY LARGE EXCAVATING MACHINERY

Machine and cost data	Capital cost £833 300	
	Dragline	Shovel
Bucket capacity, m³ (yd³)	26·74 (35)	34·38 (45)
Maximum digging depth/height, m (ft)	42·86 (141)	32·25 (106)
Maximum dumping height, m (ft)	21·58 (71)	24·32 (80)
Maximum dump radius, m (ft)	64·15 (211)	36·50 (120)
Working weight, kg (lb)	1 560 000	3 435 000
Bearing pressure, kg/cm² (lb/in²)	0·85 (12·1)	3·68 (52·4)
Bucket factor, %	65	70
Cycle time, sec	60	60
Operating efficiency, %	85	85
Output/scheduled hour, bank m³ (yd³)	890·82 (1 166)	1 227·75 (1 607)
Direct operating costs		
Operator/hour	£1.67	£1.67
Oiler/hour	£1.25	£1.25
Groundman/hour	£1.04	£1.04
Cost of electricity	£4.37	£4.37
Maintenance	£10.69	£16.07
Total cost/hour	£19.02	£24.05
Cost/bank, m³ (yd³)	£0.02 (3·90d)	£0.02 (3·60d)

Table 7.5. OPERATING COSTS FOR LARGE EXCAVATING MACHINERY

Machine and cost data	Capital cost £157 500	
	Dragline	Shovel
Size of bucket, m³ (yd³)	7	7
Bucket factor, %	65	70
Cycle time, sec	60	55
Operating efficiency, %	85	85
Output/scheduled hour, bank m³ (yd³)	169·54 (235)	207·04 (271)
Direct operating costs		
Operator/hour	£1.67	£1.67
Oiler/hour	£1.25	£1.25
Fuel oil	£1.87	£1.87
Lubricating oil	£0.21	£0.21
Maintenance (all phases)	£2.15	£2.82
Total cost/hour	£7.15	£7.82
Cost/bank m³ (yd³)	£0.03 (7·30d)	£0.03 (6·95d)

reasonable. The figures in Table 7.3 are suggested by a well-known machine manufacturer for faceshovels and draglines.

The charges to cover interest, insurance and taxes can vary according to method of calculation. Two of the methods in common use are as follows:

1. The average annual investment $\times$ 10%. The average annual investment is calculated using this formula:

$$\text{Average annual investment} = \frac{N+1}{2N} \times \text{Capital invested}$$

where N is the depreciation period in years.

2. $$\frac{0.03 \times \text{Delivered price}}{1000}$$

Operating Costs

The following items need to be considered under this heading:

1. Fuel oil—This can vary according to the condition of the machine and the type of work done. A rule of thumb on fuel consumption is:

$$\frac{\text{Engine horsepower}}{40} = \text{Fuel consumption, in gal/h.}$$

2. Oil and greases—this figure will vary from job to job, but one manufacturer makes the following estimate:

Diesel fuel used, gal/h	= index 100
Lubricating oil used, gal/h	= index 0.7
Hydraulic oil used, gal/h	= index 0.2
Grease used, lb/h	= index 0.3

3. Repair costs—see maintenance section.
4. Labour costs.

While the capital costs of various types of machine are readily available for comparison, the operating costs are not. The only figures which we have found relating to operating costs are those of American origin shown in Tables 7.4 and 7.5.

In an attempt to make some comparisons between the various excavators, the authors have drawn up the cost comparison shown in Table 7.6. Unfortunately, any exercise of this nature is bound to be open to criticism. Since no one is likely to operate all three machines together in identical conditions for several years the best one can hope for is to present reasonable estimates computed from such sources as are available. In Table 7.7 it has been attempted to take the exercise a stage further to take account of grant and resale values.

Table 7.6. COMPARATIVE COSTS OF VARIOUS TYPES OF EXCAVATING EQUIPMENT

	Faceshovel 1¼ yd³ capacity	Hydraulic excavator 1¼ yd³ capacity	Rubber-tyred shovel 3 yd³ capacity	Faceshovel 3¼ yd³ capacity	Hydraulic excavator 3¼ yd³ capacity	Rubber-tyred shovel 6 yd³ capacity
Capital cost, £	17 000	14 000	15 000	45 000	50 000	35 000
Depreciation period, hours	12 000	6 000	6 000	16 000	10 000	6 000
Depreciation, £/hour	1·41	2·33	2·50	2·81	5·00	5·83
Interest, insurance and taxes, £/hour	0·50	0·47	0·50	1·27	1·50	1·16
Owning cost/hour, £	1·91	2·80	3·00	4·08	6·50	6·99
Operating costs, £/hour						
Fuel/oil/greases	0·17	0·20	0·30	0·55	0·50	0·60
Operator	0·60	0·60	0·60	0·60	0·60	0·60
Repairs/maintenance	1·25	1·40	1·25	3·17	3·00	2·91
Tyres	–	–	0·35	–	–	1·10
Total operating costs, £/hour	2·02	2·20	2·50	4·32	4·10	5·21
Total cost/hour, £	3·93	5·00	5·50	8·40	10·60	12·20
Output at 90% availability, tons	150	170	150	500	550	450
Cost/ton, pence	6·25	7·10	8·80	4·00	4·65	6·50
Output averaged over machine life	125	160	150	425	475	450
Cost/ton (revised)	7·50	7·50	8·80	4·75	5·40	6·50

Repair and Maintenance Requirements

A survey of 41 excavators owned by one company revealed the following information:

Operating time	65·5%
Travelling and cable shifting	1·5%
Maintenance	11·4%
Mechanical stoppages	5·7%
Electrical stoppages	0·4%
Pit conditions	15·5%

This figure represents a serious loss of production, and tonnage throughout is the divisor when obtaining the ultimate production cost per ton.

Table 7.7. COMPARATIVE COSTS FOR FACESHOVEL AND RUBBER-TYRED SHOVEL

	Faceshovel $3\frac{1}{4}$ yd³ capacity	Rubber-tyred shovel 6 yd³ capacity
Capital cost, £	45 000	35 000
Less 40% grant, £	18 000	14 000
	27 000	21 000
Less resale value, £	7 000	14 000
Amount to be depreciated, £	20 000	7 000
Depreciation period, hours	20 000	6 000
Depreciation/hour, £	1.00	1.16
Interest, insurance, taxes/hour, £	1.27	1.16
Owning cost/hour	2.27	2.32
Operating costs, £/hour		
Fuel/oil/greases	0.55	0.60
Repairs/maintenance	3.17	2.00
Tyres	–	1.10
Operator	0.60	0.60
Total operating costs	4.32	4.30
Total owning and operating costs	6.59	6.62
Average output over life of machine, tons/hour	425	450
Cost/ton, pence	3.75	3.50

Machines are also deteriorating in condition due to poor working conditions, lack of lubrication, abuse in operation, improper adjustment, metal fatigue and accidents. The more obvious maintenance costs, such as labour, parts, lubricants, workshop facilities and management overheads, can be readily computed. However, several additional costs are more difficult to ascertain; these are: (*a*) the costs of labour which is idle when the units are not operating; (*b*) the revenue loss from loss of production; (*c*) the cost incurred on other plant affected by the breakdown; (*d*) the cost of injuries to persons through accidents caused by the failure of the unit.

Many articles have been written on maintenance schemes but perhaps it might be worth while to enumerate at this point some of the factors which affect maintenance costs.

1. The age of the machine—as a machine gets older parts wear out and failures occur. Unless great care is taken this general deterioration will be aggravated by corrosion. The graph in Figure 7.3 indicates the effect of age on maintenance costs for a ¾ yd face-shovel. Many operators are willing to use machines until they fall to pieces. By doing this they not only incur high repair costs but are losing the opportunity of purchasing up-to-date equipment, and at the same time the persistent downtime (Figure 7.4) and loss of output will increase the costs of production.

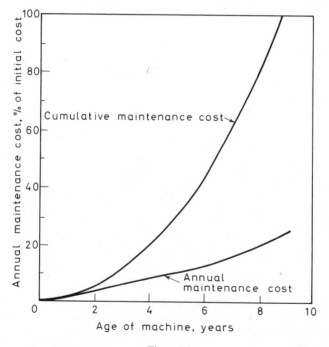

Figure 7.3

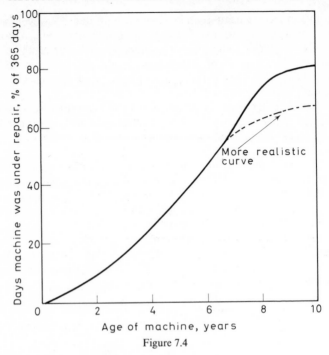

Figure 7.4

2. The scheme of maintenance in operation.
3. The type of material and the working conditions.
4. The operator.

Estimation of Maintenance Costs

Faceshovels. It should be possible to foresee these costs with reasonable accuracy provided that they are related to the economic life of the machine. The graph at Figure 7.5 shows a comparison of average maintenance costs for a wide range of machines. It will be seen that a reasonably close correlation has been achieved. One large company suggested using the following formula to give a reasonably accurate prediction of the maintenance cost:

$$\text{Maintenance cost in pence} = 10 \times \sqrt{W}$$

where W is the machine weight in tons.

However, none of these estimates takes account of the digging conditions. A leading American machine manufacturer bases the repair costs on hourly production in given conditions. A given amount of money is set against each bank yd as follows:

Easy digging	2 cents/bank yd
Medium digging	2·5 cents/bank yd
Very hard digging	3·5 cents/bank yd

This figure can then be converted as follows:

$$\text{Repair cost per ton} = \frac{\text{Cost per bank yd}}{\text{Density factor}}$$

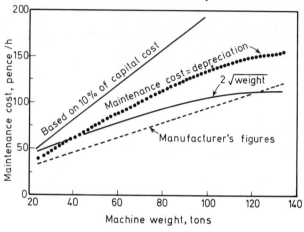

Figure 7.5

Hydraulic excavators. A major manufacturer has set out the maintenance costs as a percentage of the machine depreciation on

Table 7.8. MAINTENANCE COST FACTOR FOR HYDRAULIC EXCAVATORS

Material	Maintenance factor %
Sandy loam	50
Common earth	50
Sand	50
Gravel	50
Clay dry	60
Clay wet sticky	60
Rock well blasted:	–
basalt	65
granite	65
limestone	60
sandstone	65
shale	60
trap rock	70
Rock poorly blasted	70

its economic life for various materials, as shown in Table 7.8. One must assume that these figures are for medium digging and make some appropriate adjustment for other conditions.

Rubber-tyred shovels. A major manufacturer makes an estimate of 50 % of the hourly depreciation, but immediately states that this can be as high as 100 % of the hourly depreciation in bad conditions with poor operators and lack of preventive maintenance.

Unfortunately, the question arises as to what is meant by depreciation, since the sum to be depreciated will vary with discounts and grants available, and it must be assumed that all the manufacturers are referring to the figure to be depreciated as being the list price of the machine (less tyres in the case of the rubber-tyred shovel).

CHAPTER EIGHT

General Information

The following pages show a Form of Hire Contract and, subsequently, general conditions for the hiring of plant. These have been drawn up by the Contractors Plant Association for the guidance of members, and the authors acknowledge with gratitude the kind cooperation of the Association in permitting their reproduction in this book. Although the Form and general conditions relating to plant hire are widely known throughout the building and construction industry in the UK, it is felt that they may very well be unfamiliar in countries abroad. It is to be hoped that their publication here may serve as guidelines to those countries where plant hire is developing along similar lines to those in Britain.

In other countries outside the UK the structure of the building and construction industries differs in many respects and therefore it cannot be imagined that this Form of Hire Contract and general conditions would lend themselves to direct transposition. They would have to be modified and adapted to suit local conditions. Nevertheless, the ensuing 13 pages should at least be informative and useful if only because they are the keystone of the British planthire business and have stood the test of time and application.

Additionally, it should be borne in mind that the figures quoted here and elsewhere in this book are only approximate values to be used as a guide for comparison and have no legal significance as the basis for contract negotiation. The authors and publishers can accept no responsibility for their accuracy although, of course, every effort has been made to ensure reasonable validity at the time of writing for the comparison purposes for which they are intended. Furthermore, with the current rapid cost increases and wage rises affecting all aspects of the construction industry it is impossible to forecast what prices will be at time of publication but it may be assumed that the increases will be proportionate for both hired and purchased plant.

(To be retained by Hirer) Owner's No. ....

HIRE CONTRACT
Telephone..............

(OFFER)
Telegrams ....

....
From

(HIRER)
(OWNER)

....

....
Date of Offer

Dear Sir(s),

We thank you for your order/enquiry for hire of plant and set out below a schedule of plant which we offer to hire at the hire rates and terms noted and subject to the general conditions endorsed hereon. Acceptance of the plant on site implies acceptance of all terms and conditions stated on this offer. Please return the duplicate (acceptance) duly signed on your behalf.

Your Ref. No.	Period of Hire	From	To
*Schedule of Plant	Hire Rates and Terms		Terms of Payment
* Where interdependent items of plant are hired as a group it should be so stated or indicated by means of a bracket in the "Schedule of Plant".			

CHARGEABLE ITEMS
Operator's:—Wages
      Holiday Pay
      Insurances
      Travelling Time
      Fares
      Subsistence
        Allowance
Fuel
Oil
Grease
Consumable Stores
Insurances &c.			

Carriage or Transport of Plant:—
  To Site
  From Site			

Site(s) (exact location) Date of Delivery /19			

For and on behalf of
Owner's
Signature.......................................

N.B.—CLAUSE 13-The Hirer should cover by insurance the indemnity given to the Owner in this clause.

GENERAL CONDITIONS FOR THE HIRING OF PLANT
FORM OF CONDITIONS

1. DEFINITIONS

(a) The "Owner" is the Company, firm or person letting the plant on hire and includes their successors, assigns or personal representatives.

(b) The "Hirer" is the Company, firm, person, Corporation or public authority taking the Owner's plant on hire and includes their successors or personal representatives.

(c) "Plant" covers all classes of plant, machinery, equipment and accessories therefor which the Owner agrees to hire to the Hirer.

(d) A "day" shall be 8 hours unless otherwise specified in the Contract.

(e) A "week" shall be seven consecutive days.

(f) A "working week" covers the period from starting time on Monday to finishing time on Saturday.

Terms appearing in these conditions which also appear in any Statutory Instrument controlling rates of hire of Plant shall have the same meaning as in such instrument whether remaining in operation or not.

2. EXTENT OF CONTRACT

No conditions or warranty other than herein specifically set forth shall be implied or deemed to be incorporated in or to form part of the Contract.

3. AVAILABILITY OF PLANT

The Plant is offered subject to being available to the Owner when the Hirer's acceptance of the Contract is received by the Owner.

4. GENERAL CONDITIONS OF HIRE

Plant shall be hired at the Hire Charges or Hire Rates, so far as the same apply to Plant included in the Contract subject to the conditions of hiring provided by any Statutory Instrument controlling rates of hire of Plant and subject to the following further conditions where not inconsistent therewith.

5. LOADING AND UNLOADING

The Hirer shall be responsible for unloading and reloading the Plant at site, and any Driver, Operator or Flagman supplied by the Owner shall be deemed to be under the Hirer's control.

6. DELIVERY IN GOOD ORDER AND MAINTENANCE (INSPECTION REPORTS)

(a) Unless notification in writing to the contrary is received by the Owner from the Hirer in the case of Plant supplied with an Operator, within four working days, and in the case of

Plant supplied without Operator, within three working days of the Plant being delivered to the site, the Plant shall be deemed to be in good order in accordance with the terms of Contract and to the Hirer's satisfaction, provided that where Plant requires to be erected on site, the periods above stated shall be calculated from date of erection of Plant instead of the date of delivery on site. The Hirer shall be responsible for its safekeeping, use in a workmanlike manner within the Manufacturer's rated capacity and return on the completion of the hire in equal order (fair wear and tear excepted).

(b) The Hirer shall when hiring Plant without Owner's Operator or Driver take all reasonable steps to keep himself acquainted with the state and condition of the Plant. If Plant be continued at work or in use in an unsafe and unsatisfactory state, the Hirer shall be solely responsible for any damage, loss or accidents whether directly or indirectly arising therefrom.

(c) The current Inspection Report required under the Factories' Acts or a copy thereof shall be supplied by the Owner if requested by the Hirer at the commencement of the hire period and returned on completion thereof.

7. TIMBER MATS OR EQUIVALENTS

If the ground is soft or unsuitable for the Plant to work on or travel over without timbers or equivalents, the Hirer shall supply and lay suitable timbers or equivalents in a suitable position for the Plant to travel over or work on.

8. HANDLING OF PLANT

When a Driver or Operator is supplied by the Owner to work the Plant he shall be under the direction and control of the Hirer. Such Drivers or Operators shall for all purposes in connection with their employment in the working of the Plant be regarded as the servants or agents of the Hirer who alone shall be responsible for all claims arising in connection with the operation of the Plant by the said Drivers or Operators. The Hirer shall not allow any other person to operate such Plant without the Owner's previous consent to be confirmed in writing.

9. BREAKDOWN

(a) When the Plant is hired without Owner's Driver or Operator any breakdown or the unsatisfactory working of any part of the Plant must be notified immediately to the Owner by telegram. Any claim for breakdown time will only be considered from the time and date shown on the telegram.

(b) Full allowance will be made to the Hirer for any stoppage due to breakdown of Plant caused by the development of an inherent fault or fair wear and tear and for all stoppages for normal running repairs in accordance with the terms of the Contract.

The Hirer shall be responsible for all expense involved arising from any breakdown and all loss or damage incurred by the Owner due to the Hirer's negligence, misdirection or misuse of the Plant, whether by the Hirer or his servants, and for the payment of hire at the appropriate idle time rate during the period the Plant is necessarily idle due to such breakdown. The Owner will be responsible for the cost of repairs to the Plant involved in breakdowns from all other causes and will bear the cost of providing spare parts.

10. OTHER STOPPAGES

No claims will be admitted, other than those allowed for under Breakdown or for Idle Time, as herein provided, for stoppages through causes outside the Owner's control, including bad weather or ground conditions nor shall the Owner be responsible for the cost or expense of recovering any machine from soft ground.

11. LOSS OF USE OF OTHER PLANT DUE TO BREAKDOWN

Each item of the Plant specified in the Contract is hired as a separate unit and the breakdown or stoppage of one or more units or vehicles (whether the property of the Owner or otherwise) through any cause whatsoever, shall not entitle the Hirer to compensation or allowance for the loss of working time by any other unit or units of Plant working in conjunction therewith, provided that where two or more items of Plant are hired together as a unit, such items shall be deemed a unit for the purpose of breakdown.

12. CONSEQUENTIAL LOSS

The Owner accepts no liability nor responsibility for any consequential loss or damage due to or arising from the breakdown or stoppage of the Plant through any cause whatsoever, or through non-arrival arising from accident or breakdown during loading, unloading, or transport of the Plant.

13. HIRER'S RESPONSIBILITY FOR LOSS AND DAMAGE

During the continuance of the hire period the Hirer shall make good to the Owner all loss of or damage to the Plant from whatever cause the same may arise, fair wear and tear excepted and except as provided in Clause 9 herein, and shall also fully and completely indemnify the Owner in respect of all claims by any person whatsoever for injury to person or property caused by or in connection with or arising out of the use of the Plant and in respect of all costs and charges in connection therewith whether arising under statute or common law.

14. NOTICE OF ACCIDENTS

If the Plant is involved in any accident resulting in injury to persons or damage to property, immediate notice must be given to the Owner by telegram and confirmed in writing to the Owner's Office, and in respect of any claim not within the Hirer's agreement for indemnity, no admission, offer, promise of payment or indemnity shall be made by the Hirer without the Owner's consent in writing.

15. SUB-LETTING

The Hirer shall not sub-let or lend the Plant or any part thereof to any third party without first receiving the written permission of the Owner.

16. CHANGE OF SITE

The Hirer shall not move the Plant from the site to which it was delivered or consigned unless prior consent be obtained from the Owner, such consent to be confirmed in writing.

17. SERVICING AND INSPECTION

The Hirer shall at all reasonable times allow the Owner, his Agents or his Insurers to have access to the Plant to inspect, test, adjust, repair or replace the same. So far as reasonably possible, such work will be carried out at times to suit the convenience of the Hirer.

18. REPAIRS AND ADJUSTMENTS

Except in the case of repairs undertaken by the Owner's Operator or Driver, the Hirer shall not repair or attempt to repair the Plant unless specifically authorised by the Owner. No allowance for hire charges or for the cost of repairs will be made by the Owner to the Hirer unless such repairs have been specifically authorised by the Owner. The Owner undertakes to deal with all necessary repairs as quickly as reasonably possible.

19. RETURN OF PLANT FOR REPAIRS

(1) If at any time after the date of delivery any item of the Plant the subject of this Contract is in the opinion of the Owner in need of repairs, he may stop the further use thereof until such repairs have been carried out on site, or the Owner may arrange for such Plant to be sent to a depot and in the latter event the Owner shall be entitled to replace such Plant forthwith with similar Plant, the Owner paying all transport charges involved in the

removal of such Plant to depot for repair and the delivery of the substituted Plant and the Contract shall continue as if the substituted Plant had been the subject thereof, or, alternatively, the Owner shall be entitled to determine the Contract forthwith in relation to the item of Plant involved by giving written notice to the Hirer provided that if such determination shall occur under this Clause:

(a) within three months from the date of delivery of such Plant to site the Owner shall be liable for the cost of all transport involved including that for original loading and transport to site and for reloading and return transport of such Plant, or

(b) more than three months but less than six months from the date of delivery of such Plant the Owner shall be liable only for the cost of reloading and return transport of such Plant.

Provided always that the Hirer and not the Owner shall be liable for all costs of loading and/or transport if the necessity for such repairs arises from the negligence, misdirection or misuse of such Plant by the Hirer.

(2) In the event of this Contract being determined as aforesaid in relation to any item of Plant being the principal member of a plant group as so defined or indicated in the Schedule of Plant forming part of this Contract, of which the remaining members are auxiliary to such principal member the determination shall (unless otherwise agreed between the Owner and the Hirer) be in respect of the whole of the members of such group and the expression "such Plant" in Paragraphs (a) and (b) of sub-clause (1) of this Clause shall be construed accordingly.

20. BASIS OF CHARGING

(a) The Hirer shall render to the Owner for each working week an accurate statement of the number of hours the Plant has worked each day and where the Plant is accompanied by the Owner's Driver or Operator shall sign the Employee's Time Record Sheets daily or weekly if so requested by the Owner. The signature of the Hirer or his representative shall bind the Hirer to accept the hours shown on the Time Record Sheets. If the Hirer signs the Time Record Sheets showing hours engaged in excess of the machine hours worked plus allowed greasing time, the Hirer shall specify in detail how the extra hours are made up, otherwise the excess hours will be charged to the Hirer.

(b) Where breakdown time is referred to herein, all breakdown periods are covered which involve the Plant being inoperative through mechanical breakdown or absence of Driver or

Operator supplied by the Owner except where breakdown is due to the Hirer's misuse, misdirection or negligence.

(c) Breakdown time shall be allowed for not exceeding 8 hours on Monday to Friday and 4 hours on Saturday less the actual daily hours worked, provided that breakdown time shall not be allowed on Sundays.

(d) Plant shall be hired out at "per day" or "per week" or "per hour" for a minimum period, for a day of 8 hours or for a week of 44 hours or such other period as may be mutually agreed between the Owner and the Hirer. In the case of Plant hired "per week" for a minimum period, odd days at the beginning and at the end of the hire period shall be charged *pro rata.*

(e) Reasonable stoppages due to changing of equipment and ropes shall be charged at idle time rates.

(f) Stoppages due to changing of tyres and repairs to punctures will be chargeable as working time up to a maximum of 2 hours for any one stoppage and any excess will be treated as breakdown time.

(g) In the case of Plant which requires to be dismantled for the purposes of transportation, if the Owner agrees to a modification of the hire charge for the period required for assembling on site and dismantling upon completion of hire, such modification of the hire charge and the period for which it shall apply shall be stated on the Hire Contract.

21. PLANT HIRED ON A DAILY BASIS WITHOUT QUALIFICATION AS TO HOURS

The full daily rate will be charged on a daily basis irrespective of the hours worked except in the case of a breakdown for which the Owner is responsible, when the actual hours worked will be charged *pro rata* to the average working day. No hire charge shall be made for Sunday unless the Plant is actually worked on that day.

22. PLANT HIRED BY THE WEEK OR MONTH WITHOUT QUALIFICATION AS TO HOURS

The weekly or monthly rate shall be charged irrespective of the number of hours worked, except in the case of breakdown for which the Owner is responsible, when an allowance at the rate of two-elevenths of the agreed weekly rate or one twenty-fourth of the agreed monthly rate will be made for each full working day broken down calculated to the nearest half working day. No allowance will be made for breakdowns on Sundays.

23. **PLANT HIRED BY THE WEEK OR THE HOUR FOR A MINIMUM OF 44 HOURS PER WEEK OR A DAY OF 8 HOURS**

If no breakdown occurs, the full Hire Rate for the minimum period in the Contract will be charged and an additional *pro rata* charge will be made for hours worked in excess of such minimum period. The stipulated minimum number of hours can be worked at any time during the minimum period of a week. Allowance will be made for breakdowns up to 8 hours for a weekday and 4 hours for Saturday, providing always that where the actual hours worked are in excess of the minimum period less breakdown time, the actual hours worked shall be chargeable. Idle Time for this purpose shall be treated as actual working time. No breakdown allowance will be made for Sundays and only actual time worked charged. The minimum week of 44 hours shall be reduced by 8 hours Monday to Friday, 4 hours on Saturday, for each day's Statutory holiday occurring in such week, provided that the Plant be not worked on the holiday.

24. **"ALL-IN" RATES**

The Owner may, by arrangement with the Hirer charge "all-in" rates covering Operator's wages and insurances, holiday pay, lubricating oil, grease and consumable stores (e.g., ropes, etc.) on the basis of the minimum period. If this method be adopted time in excess of the minimum period will be charged *pro rata* plus extra wages properly paid to Operators at overtime rates.

25. **COMMENCEMENT AND TERMINATION OF HIRE (Transport of Plant)**

(a) The hire period shall commence from the time when the Plant leaves the Owner's depot or place where last employed and shall continue until the Plant is received back at the Owner's named depot or equal, but an allowance shall be made of not more than one day's hire charge each way for travelling time. If the Plant be used on day of travelling, full Hire Rates shall be paid for the period of use on that day. If more than one day be properly and unavoidably occupied in transporting the Plant, a Hire charge at Idle Time rates shall be payable for such extra time, provided that where Plant is hired for a total period of less than one week, the full Hire Rate shall be paid from the date of despatch to the date of return to the Owner's named depot or equal.

(b) Idle Time rates shall be paid for the time spent in travelling to a site other than that specified in the Contract where consent to such transfer has been given by the Owner under

Clause 16, provided that the Plant is moved by means other than under its own power.

(c) Where a road roller or other Plant travels under its own power, time properly and unavoidably spent in travelling shall be paid for as working time at full Hire Rates.

26. NOTICE OF TERMINATION OF CONTRACT

Where the period of hire is indeterminate or having been defined becomes indeterminate the Contract shall be determinable by seven days' notice in writing by either party to the other. In the event of the Hirer desiring to terminate the Contract and failing to give such notice hire for the period of the seven days' notice shall be chargeable at Idle Time rates in lieu. Notice given by the Hirer to the Owner's Driver or Operator shall not be deemed to constitute compliance with the provisions of this Clause.

27. IDLE TIME

When Plant works for any time during a guaranteed minimum period, then the whole of that guaranteed minimum period shall be charged as working time. If the Plant is idle for the whole of a guaranteed minimum period, the charge shall be at two-thirds of the Hire Rate. In any case, no period of less than one day shall be reckoned as Idle Time.

28. WAGES OF DRIVERS AND OPERATORS OF PLANT

Wages of Plant Drivers or Operators for a working week, including overtime but excluding breakdown time, shall be charged and payable weekly at nett cost or an agreed estimate of nett cost in which case breakdown time will be deducted *pro rata*. In addition to such wages the Hirer shall bear the cost of weekly stamps under the holidays with pay schemes. The wages and expenses of any Flagmen for Road Rollers provided by the Owner shall be charged to the Hirer.

29. SUBSISTENCE ALLOWANCE

The weekly subsistence allowance where paid by the Owner to his Operator shall be charged in full and is not dependent on or subject to adjustment for hours worked (subject to Clause 31(a)).

30. GREASING AND CLEANING TIME

Operators' Greasing and Cleaning Time shall be paid for and be chargeable to the Hirer at standard flat rates as follows:

Tractors alone, or with Scrapers, Bulldozers, Angledozers, etc. ..	10 hours per week
Excavators	10 ,, ,, ,,
Mechanical Trenchers	10 ,, ,, ,,
Dumpers	6 ,, ,, ,,
Compressors	6 ,, ,, ,,

(Subject to Clause 31(a)).

31. TRAVELLING TIME AND FARES

Reasonable daily travelling time and fares for Operators, similar expenses incurred at the beginning and end of the hire period and, where appropriate, the Operator's return fare to his home every six weeks will be chargeable at nett cost. No charges shall be made by the Owner for any such expenses incurred by other employees of the Owner for the purpose of servicing, repair or maintenance of Plant, unless necessitated by the Hirer's negligence, misdirection or misuse of the Plant. (Subject to Clause 31(a).)

31(a). Where Plant is broken down for seven or more consecutive days no charge shall be made under Clauses 29, 30 and 31 in respect of a Driver or Operator during period of breakdown unless alternative temporary employment be provided by the Hirer for such Driver or Operator.

32. LABOUR ON REPAIRS

The cost of labour on repairs performed by the Owner's Operators in excess of normal greasing time shall be borne by the Owner except where such repairs are necessitated by the Hirer's negligence, misdirection or misuse of the Plant.

33. FUEL, OIL AND GREASE

Fuel, Oil and Grease shall, when supplied by the Owner, be charged at nett cost or an agreed estimate of nett cost, and when supplied by the Hirer, shall be of a grade or type specified by the Owner.

34. SHARPENING OF DRILLS

Where drills or road-breakers are included with Plant hired under the Contract the Hire Rate is based upon the condition that the Hirer shall sharpen drills or road-breakers as required at his own expense.

35. CONSUMABLE STORES

Consumable stores will be charged at nett cost or an agreed estimate thereof.

36. TRANSPORT

The Hirer shall pay the cost of, and if required by the Owner, arrange transport of the Plant from the Owner's depot or equal to the site and return to named depot or equal on completion of the hire period.

37. INSURANCE

The cost of the Owner's proportion of National Insurance Contributions for the Operators supplied, and of cover against Common Law liability shall be charged at nett cost or an agreed estimate thereof.

38. OWNER PLATES

The Owner may affix his plate or mark on the Plant indicating that it is his property and the Hirer shall not remove, deface or cover up the same.

39. GOVERNMENT REGULATIONS

The Hirer will be responsible for compliance with all regulations issued by the Government or Local Authorities, including Regulations under the Factories Acts, and observance of the Road Traffic Acts should they apply, including the cost of Road Fund licences and any special additional insurances made necessary thereby, save that if and during such time as the Plant is travelling whether for full or part journey from Owner to site and site to Owner under its own power with a Driver supplied by the Owner, the Owner and not the Hirer shall be responsible as aforesaid.

40. PROTECTION OF OWNER'S RIGHTS

(a) The Hirer shall not re-hire, sell, mortgage, charge, pledge, part with possession of or otherwise deal with the Plant except as provided under Clause 15 and shall protect the same against distress, execution or seizure and shall indemnify the Owner against all losses, damage, costs, charges and expenses that may be occasioned by any failure to observe and perform this Condition, except in the event of Government requisition.

(b) If the Hirer shall make default in punctual payment of all sums due to the Owner for Hire of Plant or other charges or shall fail to observe and perform the terms and conditions of this Contract, or if the Hirer shall suffer any distress or execution to be levied against him or make or propose to make any arrangement with his creditors or being a Company, shall go into liquidation (other than a members' voluntary liquidation) or shall do or shall cause to be done or permit or suffer any act or thing whereby the Owner's rights in the Plant may be prejudiced or put into jeopardy, this Agreement shall forthwith be terminated (without any notice or other act on the part of the Owner and notwithstanding that the Owner may have waived some previous default or matter of the same or a like nature) and it shall thereupon be lawful for the Owner to retake possession of the said Plant and for that purpose to enter into or upon any premises where the same may be and the determination of the hiring under this Condition shall not affect the right of the Owner to recover from the Hirer any monies due to the Owner under the Contract or damages for breach thereof.

41. ARBITRATION

If during the Continuance of the Contract or at any time there-
after any dispute, difference or question shall arise between the
Owner and the Hirer in regard to the Contract or the Construction of these Conditions or anything therein contained or
the rights or liabilities of the Owner or the Hirer such dispute,
difference or question shall be referred pursuant to the Arbitra- •
tion Act 1950, or the Arbitration (Scotland) Act 1894 as the case
may be or any Statutory modification thereof, to a Sole Arbitrator
to be agreed upon by the Owner and the Hirer and failing agreement to be appointed at the request of either the Owner or the
Hirer by the President for the time being of the Institution of
Mechanical Engineers.

**42. PROVISIONS FOR 5-DAY WEEK OR CHANGES OF
NORMAL WEEK**

The foregoing provisions having been framed upon the basis of
the Hirer working a $5\frac{1}{2}$-day week of 44 hours it is hereby agreed
that in the event of

(a) there being any change in the normal weekly working hours
in the Industry in which the Hirer is engaged, or

(b) the Contract being made with reference to a 5-day week
being worked by the Hirer (either of 44 hours or of such
number of hours as may constitute the normal working
week in the said Industry)

Clauses 1 (d) and (f), 20 (c) and (d), 22, and (in regard to breakdown allowance and reduction for statutory holidays) 23, shall
be deemed to be modified conformably and in the event of an
alteration in the normal weekly working hours in the said
Industry the "Hire Rates and Terms" of Plant hired for a minimum weekly or daily period shall be varied *pro rata*.

43. In the event of any item or items of the Plant comprised in this
Hire Contract being used by the Hirer on or in connection with
a Contract for the construction of works or buildings and of a
forfeiture of such Contract being made by the Employer there-
under the Owner will upon request in writing made by the Employer within seven days after the date when such forfeiture has
become effective and on such Employer undertaking to pay all
Hire Charges therefor from such last mentioned date hire such
item or items to such Employer for the remainder of the period
during which such items were hired to the Hirer upon the same
terms in all respects as are herein contained save that notwithstanding the provisions of Clause 40 hereof such Employer shall
be entitled to permit the use thereof by any other contractor
employed by him for the purpose of completing the works or
buildings comprised in such Contract.

SPECIAL CONDITIONS APPLICABLE TO LORRY-MOUNTED CRANES

A. RESPONSIBILITY FOR LOSS OR DAMAGE TO GOODS BEING HANDLED

The Owner accepts no responsibility whatsoever for loss or damage to goods being handled.

B. TRAVELLING TO AND FROM SITE

Notwithstanding any clause to the contrary in this contract—

(i) **Travelling Time**—to and from the site is chargeable at full hire rate.

(ii) **Erection and Dismantling of jibs**—all time spent is chargeable at full hire rate.

(iii) **Transport of jib sections**—the transport of additional jib sections to and from the site is chargeable at extra cost.

C. SLINGS

(i) The owner will supply his standard selection of slings and no responsibility is accepted for loss or delay if these are found to be unsuitable for the purpose required.

(ii) The owner does not accept responsibility for the correct use of slings or for the method of slinging.

D. CONSEQUENTIAL DAMAGE

No responsibility is accepted for damage to property beneath the wheels of the vehicle or to any overhead obstructions.

E. SITE CONDITIONS

Your attention is drawn to Clause 7 of the General Conditions for the Hiring of Plant—it is the Hirer's responsibility for the adequacy of the ground (or timbers) to support the crane under its wheels and outriggers.

F. HANDLING OF PLANT

Your attention is drawn to Clause 8 of the General Conditions for the Hiring of Plant, the crane being supplied to work within its capacity under your supervision.

Cost Comparisons

Type of machine*	Approx. purchase cost 1970	Approx. value after 5 years	CPA hire rate† based on min. 40-h week (1970)	Approx. hire cost over 5 years based on 30-week year
10/7 concrete mixer c/w weigh gear and loader	£1 500	£180	£18.50	£2 775
Vibrating plate compactor	£533	w.o.	£6.33	£950
Compressors				
100–150 c.f.m.	£1 400	£250	£15.25	£2 285
151–250 c.f.m.	£2 500	£450	£27	£4 050
Cranes (mobile)				
4 ton	£4 000	£900	£40	£6 000
10 ton	£9 968	£3 000	£114	£17 100
Cranes (lorry-mounted)				
25 ton	£29 500	£6 500	£290	£43 500
60 ton	£42 500	£9 000	£660	£99 000
Dumpers				
1 yd^3	£492	£70	£14	£2 100
2 yd^3	£775	£150	£17.50	£2 625
Dumptrucks				
6 yd^3	£5 500	£900	£72	£10 800
Excavators (rope)				
$\frac{3}{4}$ yd^3	£9 000	£3 500	£65.50	£9 750
Excavators (hydraulic)	£8 600	£3 000	£90	£13 500
Motor grader				
113–132 h.p.	£13 000	£3 500	£94.50	£14 175
150 h.p.	£16 500	£4 500	£120	£18 000
Piling hammers (diesel)				
K.E. 12 000 ft lb	£2 750	£1 000	£60	£9 000
16 800 ft lb	£2 800	£1 000	£75	£11 250
24 000 ft lb	£4 600	£1 500	£85	£12 750
Pumps (water) diaphragm				
3 in	£250	£50	£9.50	£1 425
4 in	£450	£75	£11.50	£1 725
centrifugal				
3 in	£525	£50	£9.50	£1 425
4 in	£700	£100	£12.65	£1 897.50
6 in	£1 240	£200	£17.70	£2 805

COST COMPARISONS—*continued*

Type of machine*	Approx. purchase cost 1970	Approx. value after 5 years	CPA hire rate† based on min. 40-h week (1970)	Approx. hire cost over 5 years based on 30-week year
Road rollers, 3-point				
over 5 ton	£2 500	£500	£34	£5 100
over 8 ton	£3 500	£850	£36	£5 400
over 10 ton	£4 500	£1 500	£38	£5 700
Towed vibratory roll width				
54 in	£2 305	£450	£11.50	£1 725
72 in	£2 325	£450	£30	£4 500
75 in	£2 525	£500	£32	£4 800
Concrete pumps				
4 in	£17 000	£2 500	£350	£43 750 based on 25-week year
Scrapers (motor)				
14–18 yd³	£20 000	£5 000	£231	£34 650
18–24 yd³	£33 000	£8 500	£286	£42 900
24–31 yd³	£42 000	£12 000	£429	£65 000
32–44 yd³	£81 700	£20 000	£600	£90 000
Shovels (loading) **2-wheel drive**				
70–90 h.p. (1–1½ yd³)	£3 850	£1 000	£50.67	£7 600
90–120 h.p. (1¾–2¼ yd³)	£4 500	£1 250	£60	£9 000
4-wheel drive				
80–85 h.p. (1¾–2 yd³)	£7 000	£2 000	£50	£7 500
110–130 h.p. (2½–4 yd³)	£8 400	£2 300	£120	£18 000
210–250 h.p. (5–6 yd³)	£22 560	£6 000	£200	£30 000
Tractors				
45–65·9 h.p.	£6 500	£1 200	£50	£7 500
90–140 h.p.	£13 000	£3 500	£136	£20 400
180–210 h.p.	£19 000	£4 500	£176	£26 400
240–310 h.p.	£23 000	£7 000	£240	£36 000
Traxcavators				
1 yd³	£9 600	£1 500	£80	£12 000
1½ yd³	£12 000	£3 000	£118.80	£17 820
1¾ yd³	£13 200	£3 500	£120	£18 000
2½ yd³	£20 000	£4 000	£178	£26 700
3 yd³	£24 000	£5 000	£202	£30 360
5 yd³	£34 400	£7 500	£260	£39 000

* Hire rates for machines do not include operator.
† The hire rates issued by the CPA were based on 1968 capital values and therefore, in many instances, present-day values should be increased by something more than 25 % throughout the range, to allow for increased maintenance and replacement costs.

General Earthmoving Information

Performance of earthmoving equipment is measured by comparing the hourly machine productivity and the machine hourly owning and operating cost. Optimum machine performance can be expressed as:

$$\text{Top machine performance} = \frac{\text{Lowest possible hourly costs}}{\text{Highest possible hourly productivity}}$$

Production is the hourly rate at which material is moved. Production can be expressed in various units:

Bank cubic yards, BCY (bank yd³)
Loose cubic yards, LCY (loose yd³)
Compacted cubic yards, CCY (compacted yd³)
Bank cubic metres, BM³ (bank m³)
Loose cubic metres, LM³ (loose m³)
Compacted cubic metres, CM³ (compacted m³)
Tons (English short tons or metric tonnes)

For most earthmoving and material-handling applications, production is calculated by multiplying the quantity of material moved per cycle by the number of cycles per hour:

$$\text{Production} = \text{Load/cycle} \times \text{Cycles/h}$$

The load can be determined by: (a) load weighing; (b) load estimating; (c) cross-section of cut or fill.

Volume Measure

Soil volume is defined according to its state in the earthmoving process. The three measures of soil volume are:

BCY (BM³)—1 yd³ (m³) of material as it lies in the natural state.
LCY (LM³)—1 yd³ (m³) of material which has been disturbed and
swelled as a result of loading.
CCY (CM³)—1 yd³ (m³) of material which has been compacted
and has shrunk as a result of compaction.

Assume 1·0 BCY of material weighs 3000 lb. By virtue of the material characteristics this BCY swells to 1·3 yd³ when loaded. The resulting 1·3 LCY weighs 3000 lb and has 30% swell. If the 1·0 BCY or 1·3 LCY is compacted, its volume may be reduced to 0·8 yd³. The BCY has therefore been reduced to 0·8 CCY, still with a weight of 3000 lb.

Generally, earthmoving jobs are calculated on the basis of BCY. Thus in order to estimate production, the relationships between bank measure, loose measure and compacted measure must be known.

The ratio between bank measure and loose measure is called load factor (LF):

$$LF = \frac{BCY}{LCY}$$

Load factor may also be obtained, if the percentage of swell of the material is known, by using the following relationship:

$$LF = \frac{100\%}{100\% + \% \text{ swell}}$$

To estimate the machine payload in BCY, the volume in loose cubic yards is multiplied by the load factor:

$$\text{Load (BCY)} = \frac{CCY}{BCY}$$

Shrinkage factor is either estimated or obtained from job plans or specifications which show the conversion from compacted measure to bank measure. Shrinkage factor should not be confused with percentage compaction (used for specifying embankment density, such as Modified Proctor or CBR).

Example

Construct a 10 000 yd³ bridge approach of dry clay with a shrinkage factor of 0·80. Haul unit is rated 14 yd³ struck and 20 yd³ heaped. How many bank yards are needed and how many loads are required?

$$BCY = \frac{CCY}{SF} = \frac{10\,000}{0·80} = 12\,500$$

$$\text{Load BCY} = LCY \times LF = 20 \times 0·72 = 14·4\,BCY$$

(LF of 0·72 from Tables)

$$\text{Number of loads required} = \frac{12\,500}{14·4} = 869$$

Calculation Guides for Earthmoving Plant Operation

Production, hourly $= \text{Load (BCY)/cycle} \times \text{Cycles/h}$
$= \text{Load (BM}^3\text{)/cycle} \times \text{Cycles/h}$

Load factor (LF) $= \frac{BCY}{LCY} = \frac{BM^3}{LM^3}$

Load factor (LF) $= \frac{100\%}{100\% + \% \text{ swell}}$

Load (bank measure) $= LCY \times LF = LM^3 \times LF$

Shrinkage factor (SF) $= \dfrac{\text{CCY}}{\text{BCY}} = \dfrac{\text{CM}^3}{\text{BM}^3}$

Density $=$ Weight/Unit volume

Load (bank measure) $= \dfrac{\text{Weight of load}}{\text{Bank density}}$

Rolling resistance factor $= 40$ lb/ton $+ (30$ lb/ton/in $\times$ in)
$\qquad\qquad\qquad\qquad = 20$ kg/tonne $+ (15$ kg/tonne/2·5 cm $\times$ cm)

Rolling resistance $=$ RR factor (lb/ton) $\times$ GVW (ton)
$\qquad\qquad\qquad = $ RR factor (kg/tonne) $\times$ GVW (tonne)

Rolling resistance $= 2\%$ of GVW $+ 1·5\%$ of GVW per inch tyre
$\qquad\qquad\qquad$ penetration.
$\qquad\qquad\quad = 2\%$ of GVW $+ 0·6\%$ of GVW per cm tyre
$\qquad\qquad\qquad$ penetration.

Grade resistance factor $= 20$ lb/ton $\times \%$ grade
$\qquad\qquad\qquad\qquad = 10$ kg/tonne $\times \%$ grade

Grade resistance $=$ GR factor (lb/ton) $\times$ GVW (ton)
$\qquad\qquad\qquad = $ GR factor (kg/tonne) $\times$ GVW (tonne)

Grade resistance $= 1\%$ of GVW $\times \%$ grade

Total resistance $=$ Rolling resistance (lb or kg) $+$ Grade resistance
$\qquad\qquad\qquad\qquad\qquad\qquad\qquad\qquad\qquad$ (lb or kg)

Rolling resistance $(\%) = 2\% + 1·5\%$ per inch tyre penetration
$\qquad\qquad\qquad\quad = 2\% + 0·6\%$ per cm tyre penetration

Grade resistance $(\%) = \%$ grade

Effective grade $(\%) = $ RR $(\%) +$ GR $(\%)$

Usable pull (traction limitation)
$\qquad = $ Coeff. of traction $\times$ Weight on drivers
$\qquad = $ Coeff. of traction $\times$ (Total wt. $\times \%$ on drivers)

Pull required $=$ Rolling resistance $+$ Grade resistance $=$ Total resis-
$\qquad\qquad\qquad\qquad\qquad\qquad\qquad\qquad\qquad\qquad$ tance

Total cycle time $=$ Fixed time $+$ Variable time

Variable time $=$ Total haul time $+$ Total return time

Travel time $= \dfrac{\text{Distance (ft)}}{\text{Speed (ft/min)}} = \dfrac{\text{Distance (m)}}{\text{Speed (m/min)}}$

Cycles per hour $= \dfrac{60 \text{ min}}{\text{Total cycle time (min)}}$

Adjusted prod. $=$ Hourly prod. $\times$ Efficiency factor

No. of units required $= \dfrac{\text{Hourly prod. required}}{\text{Unit hourly production}}$

No. of scrapers a pusher will load $= \dfrac{\text{Scraper cycle time}}{\text{Pusher cycle time}}$

Vehicle Performance Limiting Factors

Conditions such as haul road profile, haul road condition, and vehicle weight determine how delivered power becomes vehicle performance.

Rolling Resistance

Rolling resistance (abbreviated Ro. Ri.) is a measure of the force required to overcome internal friction of the bearings and, on rubber-tyred units, to overcome the retarding effect between the tyres and the ground. This includes the resistance caused by the penetration of the tyres into the ground and by the flexing of the tyre under load. Track-type tractive force is delivered to a set of steel tracks and thus there is no penetration or flexing. The internal friction of a crawler tractor includes the friction of rotating the track chain and is already deducted from crawler drawbar pull charts. Rolling resistance may be expressed in terms of pounds or percentage. For example, a resistance of 40 lb/ton of vehicle weight is 2% rolling resistance.

$$\frac{40 \text{ lb force required}}{2000 \text{ lb vehicle weight}} = 2\%$$

An 80 000 lb vehicle on a level road with a rolling resistance of 2% must develop 1600 lb of rimpull (80 000 × 2%) to overcome resistance before it starts to move. If 20 000 lb of rimpull were available at 5 m.p.h. then 18 400 lb of drawbar pull (20 000 lb—1600 lb) would be available to do work.

The weight of a vehicle determines the force required to overcome the rolling and grade resistances. The pulling force remaining after losses for total resistance have been subtracted, is then available for acceleration.

For example, if the rolling resistance were 2% and the grade resistance 6%, the vehicle must develop 6400 lb of rimpull to overcome a total resistance of 8% (80 000 × 8%). Of the 20 000 lb of rimpull originally available, 13 600 lb would be available for acceleration (20 000 lb—6400 lb).

Traction

A spinning wheel or track does not deliver power to the ground. The two factors which keep a wheel or track from spinning are the weight it carries and the traction available from the ground conditions. The degree of traction between the tyre or track shoe and the ground is called the coefficient of traction. Since there is never 100% adhesion, the coefficient is always less than 1·0. The result of multiplying the weight on the drive axle, or the weight of the entire machine in the case of a track-type unit, times the coefficient of traction, represents the maximum force which can be transmitted before the track or tyre spins out.

For example, a vehicle with 50 000 lb on the drive axle, working on a ground condition with a coefficient of traction of 0·6, can deliver up to 30 000 lb (50 000 × 0·6) of rimpull before the tyre will spin out.

All-wheel drive vehicles and crawler tractors have 100% of the vehicle's weight on the drive axle and thus are capable of delivering

Table 8.1

Ground surface	Rolling resistance %
Asphalt	1·5
Concrete	1·5
Dirt	
smooth, hard, dry; well maintained; free of loose material	2.0
dry, but not firmly packed; some loose material	3·0
soft, unploughed; poorly maintained	4·0
soft, ploughed	8·0
unpacked fills	8·0
deeply rutted	16·0
Gravel	
well compacted; dry; free of loose material	2·0
not firmly compacted; but dry	3·0
loose	10·0
Mud	
with firm base	4·0
with soft spongy base	16·0
Sand	
loose	10·0
packed	2·5
to 4 in depth; loose	4·5

more of the rimpull available than are single-drive axle vehicles. Table 8.1 shows the common coefficient of traction for various ground conditions.

The ability of rubber-tyred vehicles to deliver power may be altered on extremely slippery ground or where extremely steep grades cause weight to be transferred on to or off the drive axle.

Coefficient of Traction

Materials	Rubber tyres	Tracks
Concrete	0·90	0·45
Clay loam, dry	0·55	0·90*
Clay loam, wet	0·45	0·70
Rutted clay loam	0·40	0·70
Dry sand	0·20	0·30
Wet sand	0·40	0·50
Quarry pit	0·65	0·55
Gravel road (loose)	0·35	0·50
Dry packed snow	0·40	0·50
Ice	0·10	0·10
Firm earth	0·60	0·90*
Loose earth	0·45	0·60

*Assumes full grouser penetration.

Travel Time Conversion in Minutes

Speed m.p.h.	Travel distance, ft									
3	0·379	0·757	1·136	1·515	1·893	2·272	2·65	3·03	3·41	3·79
4	0·284	0·568	0·853	1·136	1·42	1·70	2·00	2·27	2·55	2·84
5	0·227	0·454	0·681	0·908	1·136	1·363	1·59	1·82	2·04	2·27
6	0·189	0·378	0·568	0·757	0·946	1·136	1·325	1·51	1·70	1·89
7	0·162	0·324	0·487	0·649	0·811	0·974	1·136	1·30	1·46	1·62
8	0·142	0·284	0·426	0·568	0·710	0·852	0·994	1·136	1·28	1·42
9	0·126	0·252	0·378	0·505	0·631	0·757	0·883	1·00	1·136	1·26
10	0·113	0·227	0·341	0·454	0·568	0·681	0·795	0·909	1·02	1·136
12·5	0·091	0·182	0·273	0·363	0·454	0·545	0·636	0·727	0·818	0·909
15	0·075	0·151	0·227	0·303	0·378	0·454	0·530	0·605	0·681	0·757
17·5	0·065	0·129	0·194	0·259	0·324	0·389	0·454	0·519	0·584	0·649
20	0·057	0·113	0·170	0·227	0·284	0·341	0·397	0·454	0·511	0·568
22·5	0·050	0·101	0·151	0·202	0·252	0·303	0·353	0·404	0·454	0·505
25	0·045	0·090	0·136	0·181	0·227	0·272	0·317	0·363	0·408	0·454
27·5	0·041	0·082	0·124	0·165	0·206	0·248	0·289	0·330	0·371	0·412
30	0·038	0·076	0·113	0·151	0·189	0·227	0·265	0·303	0·341	0·379
32·5	0·035	0·070	0·104	0·139	0·174	0·209	0·244	0·279	0·314	0·349
35	0·032	0·065	0·097	0·129	0·162	0·194	0·227	0·259	0·291	0·324

Example

To find the required time to travel 750 ft at 9 m.p.h.

$$700 \text{ ft at } 9 \text{ m.p.h.} = 0.883$$

50 ft $= \frac{1}{2}$ time shown for 100 ft travel: 50 ft at 9 m.p.h. $= \underline{0.063}$

$$\overline{0.946} \text{ min}$$

Enter 0·95 min as travel time for 750 ft at 9 m.p.h.

$$\text{Travel time in minutes} = \frac{\text{Distance in feet}}{\text{m.p.h.} \times 88}$$

$$\text{Miles per hour} = \frac{\text{Distance in feet}}{\text{Travel time in minutes} \times 88}$$

Material Weights

Material	Weight in BCY	Weight in LCY
Ashes, hard coal	700–1 000 lb	650– 930 lb
Ashes, soft coal with clinkers	1 000–1 515 lb	930–1 410 lb
Ashes, soft coal, ordinary	1 080–1 215 lb	1 000–1 130 lb
Bauxite	2 700–4 325 lb	2 020–3 240 lb
Brick	–	2 700 lb
Cement, Portland	94 lb per bag	–
Cement, Portland	2 970 lb (packed)	2 450 lb
Clay, dry	2 300 lb	1 840 lb
Clay, light	2 800 lb	2 160 lb
Clay, dense, tough, or wet	3 000 lb	2 250 lb
Coal, anthracite	2 200 lb	1 630 lb
Coal, bituminous	1 900 lb	1 400 lb
Coke, lump, loose	–	620–865 lb
Coke, solvay, egg, chestnut or pea	–	840 lb
Coke, gas, egg, chestnut or pea	–	785 lb
Coke, gas furnace	–	730 lb
Concrete	3 240–4 185 lb	2 330–3 000 lb
Concrete, mix wet	–	3 500–3 750 lb
Copper ore	3 800 lb	2 800 lb
Earth, dry	2 800 lb	2 240 lb
Earth, wet	3 370 lb	2 700 lb
Earth with sand and gravel	3 100 lb	2 640 lb
Earth and rock mixture, such as unclassified excavation	2 500–3 000 lb	1 920–2 310 lb
Gravel, dry	3 250 lb	2 900 lb
Gravel, wet	3 600 lb	3 200 lb
Granite	4 500 lb	3 000–2 520 lb
Iron ore, hematite	6 500–8 700 lb	3 900 lb
Iron ore, limonite	6 400 lb	–
Iron ore, magnetite	8 500 lb	–
Kaolin	2 800 lb	2 160 lb
Lead ore, galina	12 550 lb	–
Lime	–	1 400 lb
Limestone, blasted	4 200 lb	2 400–2 520 lb
Limestone, loose, crushed	–	2 600–2 700 lb
Limestone, marble	4 600 lb	2 620–2 760 lb
Loam	2 700 lb	2 240 lb
Mud, dry (close)	2 160–2 970 lb	1 790–2 460 lb
Mud, wet (moderately packed)	2 970–3 510 lb	2 470–2 910 lb
Oil, crude	6·42 lb/gal	–
Phosphate rock	5 400 lb	–
Rock, hard, well blasted	4 000 lb	2 680 lb
Rock and stone, crushed	3 240–3 920 lb	2 400–2 900 lb
Shale or soft rock	3 000 lb	2 250 lb

MATERIAL WEIGHTS—*continued*

Material	Weight in BCY	Weight in LCY
Sand, dry	3 250 lb	2 900 lb
Sand, wet	3 600 lb	3 200 lb
Sandstone	4 140 lb	2 980–2 610 lb
Shale, riprap	2 800 lb	2 100 lb
Slag, sand	1 670 lb	1 485 lb
Slag, solid	4 320–4 860 lb	3 240–2 640 lb
Slag, crushed	–	1 900 lb
Slag, furnace, granulated	1 600 lb	1 430 lb
Slate	4 590–4 860 lb	3 530–3 740 lb
Trap rock	5 075 lb	3 400 lb
Wood		
beech		3 250 lb per cord
chestnut		2 350 lb per cord
elm		2 350 lb per cord
pine, Norway or white		2 000 lb per cord
poplar		2 350 lb per cord

Ton m.p.h. (km/h) Tyre Rating at Ambient Temperature °F (°C)

Tyre size in	Type	60° (16°)	80° (27°)	100° (38°)	120° (49°)
18–25	Std tread (E-3)	150 (219)	140 (204)	125 (182)	110 (161)
	Extra tread (E-4)	120 (175)	110 (161)	100 (146)	90 (131)
	Radial S.C.	210 (306)	195 (285)	175 (255)	160 (233)
18–33	Std tread (E-3)	175 (255)	155 (226)	140 (204)	120 (175)
	Extra tread (E-4)	150 (219)	140 (204)	125 (182)	110 (161)
	Radial S.C.	300 (438)	270 (394)	240 (351)	205 (299)
21–35	Std tread (E-3)	200 (291)	185 (270)	165 (241)	145 (211)
	Extra tread (E-4)	170 (248)	150 (219)	135 (197)	115 (168)
	Radial S.C.	330 (482)	300 (438)	270 (394)	235 (343)
26·5–29	Std tread (E-3)	175 (255)	155 (226)	140 (204)	120 (175)
	Radial S.C.	340 (496)	310 (452)	280 (409)	245 (358)
29·5–29	Std tread (E-3)	185 (270)	165 (241)	150 (219)	130 (190)
	Radial S.C.	400 (584)	360 (525)	320 (467)	280 (409)
29·5–35	Std tread (E-3)	215 (314)	200 (292)	180 (263)	160 (234)
	Radial S.C.	530 (773)	450 (657)	370 (540)	280 (409)
33·25–35	Std tread (E-3)	225 (328)	210 (306)	190 (277)	170 (248)
	Radial S.C.	530 (773)	480 (700)	430 (628)	380 (555)
33·5–39	Std tread (E-3)	245 (356)	215 (314)	190 (277)	160 (233)
	Radial S.C.	570 (833)	510 (745)	445 (650)	380 (555)
37·5–39	Std tread (E-3)	275 (401)	250 (365)	230 (336)	205 (299)
	Radial S.C.	580 (846)	520 (759)	455 (664)	390 (569)
37·5–51	Std tread (E-3)	290 (423)	260 (379)	230 (336)	195 (285)
	Radial S.C.	690 (1008)	620 (905)	550 (803)	480 (700)
36·00–51	Std tread (E-3)	500 (730)	440 (642)	390 (569)	350 (511)

Ton m.p.h. (km/h) rating = Mean tyre load × Workday average speed.
Tyre dealers should be consulted for their current design and ton m.p.h. rating.

Calculating for Tyre Failure

Internal heat is the main cause of premature tyre failures. Heat is generated internally in the tyre as it rolls and flexes, and when heat is generated faster than it can be conducted to the surface and radiated into the atmosphere, the temperature gradually builds up, reaching maximum at the outer ply. When tyres are overflexed, sufficient head develops and ply separation and tyre failure result.

The 'ton-mile-per-hour' formula was developed to predict tyre temperature build-up. The system is a method of rating tyres in proportion to the amount of work they can do from a temperature standpoint. It utilises the product of load times speed to derive an index of the tyre temperature build-up with maximum safe tyre level of temperatures of 225° F and 200° C being set for fabric cord tyres and steel wire cord tyres, respectively, by the tyre industry.

Heat generation in a specific tyre depends on the weight carried, the speed over the ground and the ambient temperature.

These are all specific job conditions and can be used to determine the maximum work capacity of any tyre.

Ton-mile-per-hour rating system (metric system: tonne-kilometre-per-hour—to use the following discussion and formulae in the metric system, change miles to kilometres and use metric tonnes):

Ton m.p.h. = Mean tyre load × Workday average speed

Mean Tyre Load

During the earthmoving cycle the tyre carries the empty machine and the loaded machine. Mean tyre load is the average of the empty machine weight and the loaded machine weight on the tyre:

Mean tyre load=
$$\frac{\text{Tyre load wt/Unit empty (ton)} + \text{Tyre load wt/Unit loaded (ton)}}{2}$$

In the rare case where the machine operates loaded in both directions, the mean tyre load calculation must take it into account.

Workday Average Speed

Workday average speed is the total miles travelled in a workday divided by the total hours of the workday. Total workday hours are total hours of operation in 24 h and include lunch breaks, rest periods, shift change times, etc.

$$\text{Workday average speed} = \frac{\text{Total cycle distance (miles} \times \text{Trips per workday)}}{\text{Total workday hours}}$$

For the workday average speed to be valid, it is necessary that no major deviation from the average speed occurs.

From the ton m.p.h. rating chart (p. 178), select the ambient temperature column approximating the maximum prevailing ambient temperature on the job. Opposite the correct tyre size, select a conventional or radial steel cord tyre that has a ton m.p.h. rating equal to, or slightly greater than, the calculated ton m.p.h. requirements.

The ton m.p.h. ratings given in the chart are valid only for the particular tyres at the time of testing. The manufacturers make changes in construction and compounding from time to time in an effort to improve tyre performance. Users are recommended that, at the time of purchase, they check with the tyre supplier for specific ton m.p.h. ratings of their current tyres.

Power Shovel Output (90° Swing)

LCY per 60 minute hour/LCY per minute

Bucket capacity yd	Easy digging	Medium digging	Hard digging or rock
$\frac{3}{4}$	166/ 2·77	139/ 2·32	117/ 1·95
1	214/ 3·57	178/ 2·97	152/ 2·53
$1\frac{1}{2}$	307/ 5·12	250/ 4·17	221/ 3·68
2	393/ 6·55	317/ 5·28	285/ 4·75
$2\frac{1}{2}$	480/ 8·00	379/ 6·32	344/ 5·73
3	563/ 9·38	442/ 7·37	400/ 6·66
$3\frac{1}{2}$	643/ 7·16	507/ 8·45	453/ 7·55
4	717/11·95	563/ 9·39	508/ 8·47
$4\frac{1}{2}$	791/13·18	625/10·42	559/ 9·32
5	895/14·92	684/11·40	611/10·18
$5\frac{1}{2}$	934/15·57	740/12·33	665/11·08
6	1 005/16·75	798/13·30	717/11·95
$6\frac{1}{2}$	1 075/17·92	852/14·20	771/12·85
7	1 145/19·08	923/15·38	820/13·67
8	1 280/21·33	1 030/17·17	922/15·37
9	1 425/23·75	1 150/19·16	1 030/17·17
10	1 580/26·33	1 270/21·16	1 120/18·66
11	1 720/28·66	1 380/23·00	1 220/20·33
12	1 860/31·00	1 500/25·00	1 320/22·00
13	2 000/33·33	1 610/26·83	1 420/23·66
14	2 140/35·66	1 720/28·66	1 510/25·17
15	2 290/38·16	1 830/30·50	1 610/26·83

Dragline Output (90° Swing)

LCY per 60 minute hour/LCY per minute

Bucket capacity yd	Easy digging	Medium digging	Hard digging or rock
$\frac{3}{4}$	132/ 2·20	114/ 1·90	87/ 1·45
1	168/ 2·80	144/ 2·40	111/ 1·85
$1\frac{1}{4}$	202/ 3·37	174/ 2·90	134/ 2·23
$1\frac{1}{2}$	229/ 3·82	200/ 3·33	160/ 2·67
$1\frac{3}{4}$	256/ 4·27	226/ 3·77	182/ 3·03
2	283/ 4·72	250/ 4·17	202/ 3·37
$2\frac{1}{2}$	328/ 5·47	291/ 4·85	240/ 4·00
3	363/ 6·05	322/ 5·37	268/ 4·47
$3\frac{1}{2}$	396/ 6·60	352/ 5·87	297/ 4·95
4	430/ 7·17	385/ 6·42	328/ 5·47
$4\frac{1}{2}$	468/ 7·80	420/ 7·00	360/ 6·00
5	505/ 8·42	455/ 7·58	391/ 6·52
$5\frac{1}{2}$	540/ 9·00	487/ 8·12	426/ 7·10
6	579/ 9·65	524/ 8·73	460/ 7·67
$6\frac{1}{2}$	615/10·25	572/ 9·53	494/ 8·23
7	659/10·98	595/ 9·92	530/ 8·83
8	750/12·50	672/11·20	574/ 9·57
9	839/13·98	750/12·50	678/11·30
11	1 010/16·83	900/15·00	805/13·42
13	1 190/19·83	1 050/17·50	939/15·65
15	1 360/22·67	1 190/19·83	1 070/17·83

Conversion of Cubic Yards to Cubic Metres

yd³	m³	yd³	m³	yd³	m³
$\frac{1}{2}$	0·38	33	25·23	71	54·28
1	0·76	34	25·99	72	55·05
$1\frac{1}{2}$	1·15	35	26·76	73	55·81
2	1·53	36	27·52	74	56·58
$2\frac{1}{2}$	1·91	37	28·29	75	57·34
3	2·29	38	29·05	76	58·11
$3\frac{1}{2}$	2·68	39	29·82	77	58·87
4	3·06	40	30·58	78	59·64
$4\frac{1}{2}$	3·44	41	31·35	79	60·40
5	3·82	42	32·11	80	61·16
$5\frac{1}{2}$	4·21	43	32·88	81	61·93
6	4·59	44	33·64	82	62·69
7	5·35	45	34·41	83	63·46
8	6·12	46	35·17	84	64·22
9	6·88	47	35·93	85	64·99
10	7·65	48	36·70	86	65·75
11	8·41	49	37·46	87	66·52
12	9·17	50	38·23	88	67·28
13	9·94	51	38·99	89	68·05

CUBIC YARDS TO CUBIC METRES—*continued*

yd³	m³	yd³	m³	yd³	m³
14	10·70	52	39·76	90	68·81
15	11·47	53	40·52	91	69·57
16	12·23	54	41·29	92	70·34
17	13·00	55	42·05	93	71·10
18	13·76	56	42·82	94	71·87
19	14·53	57	43·58	95	72·63
20	15·29	58	44·34	96	73·40
21	16·06	59	45·11	97	74·16
22	16·82	60	45·87	98	74·93
23	17·58	61	46·64	99	75·69
24	18·35	62	47·40	100	76·46
25	19·11	63	48·17	150	114·68
26	19·88	64	48·93	200	152·91
27	20·64	65	49·70	250	191·14
28	21·41	66	50·46	300	229·37
29	22·17	67	51·23	350	267·60
30	22·94	68	51·99	400	305·82
31	23·70	69	52·75	450	344·05
32	24·47	70	53·52	500	382·28

Conversion Factors

1 in = 25·4 mm
1 ft = 0·305 m
1 yd = 0·914 m
1 mile = 1·609 km
1 mm = 0·039 370 in
1 m = 39·370 in
$\quad$ = 3·281 ft
$\quad$ = 1·093 yd
1 km = 0·621 371 mile

1 in² = 6·452 cm²
1 yd² = 0·836 m²
1 acre (4 840 yd²) = 4 047 m²
1 hectare (10 000 m²) = 2·471 acre
1 cm² = 0·155 in²
1 m² = 1550 in²
$\quad$ = 10·764 ft²

1 in³ = 16·387 cm³
1 ft³ = 0·028 3 m³
1 yd³ = 0·764 m³
1 cm³ = 0·061 in³
1 m³ = 35·315 ft³
$\quad$ = 1·308 yd³

1 lb = 0·454 kg
1 cwt = 50·802 kg
1 UK ton (2 240 lb) = 1 016·047 kg
1 US ton (2 000 lb) = 907 kg
1 kg = 2·204 6 lb
1 tonne (1 000 kg) = 2 204·62 lb
$\quad$ = 0·984 2 UK ton

1 m³ *equals:*
2 203 lb water (1 ton, nearly)
220 UK gal (1 UK gal = 1·201 US gal)
264 US gal (1 US gal = 0·833 UK gal)

lb/in² × 0·070 3 = kg/cm²
kg/cm² × 14·223 = lb/in²
lb/ft² × 4·882 = kg/m²
kg/m² × 0·204 8 = lb/ft²
lb/yd³ × 0·593 = kg/m³
kg/m³ × 1·686 = lb/yd³
ton/yd³ × 1·329 = tonnes/m³
tonnes/m³ × 0·752 = ton/yd³
ft-ton × 0·309 = tonne metres
tonne metres × 3·23 = ft-tons

1 ft³ *equals:*
62·3 lb water
28·316 litres
0·028 3 m³
6·23 UK gal
7·48 US gal

1 UK pt = 0·568 litre
1 UK gal = 4·546 litres
1 litre = 1·76 UK pt

Index